Praise for Unexpected Allies: Men Who Stop Rape

"Todd Denny's techniques go to the heart of male ignorance about sexual violence, not to preach, but to transform -- a brilliantly nuanced and accessible approach."

-Gaetano "Guy" B. Senese, Ph.D., Professor,
Northern Arizona University.
Author of *Simulation, Spectacle and the Ironies of Education Reform.*

"Denny teaches men how to take responsibility for ending violence against women. Men who are interested in getting involved and recruiting others will benefit tremendously from this book."

-Golie Jansen, Ph.D., Grant Director,
U.S. Department of Justice project "Campus Violence Against Women",
Eastern Washington University.

"This book brings Todd Denny's dynamic, culturally-responsive voice to the world of print. He has invented novel ways to reach and teach Black, Native-American and Mexican-American youth."

-Stafford Hood, Ph.D., Dean for Research,
College of Education, Arizona State University.
Author of *The Role of Culture and Cultural Context: A Mandate for Inclusion.*

"This book offers clear and concise strategies for engaging men in innovative violence prevention programs. Read it. Better yet, use it!"

-Chandra Lindeman, Coordinator for the Office of Sexual Assault,
The Evergreen State College, Olympia, WA.

"A must read, Denny's suggestions, if acted on, would save our country untold millions of dollars and countless tortured lives in both rural and urban areas."

-L.T. Wallace, Ph.D., Extension Economist, Emeritus,
University of California, Berkeley.
Author of Agriculture, Economics and Resource Management.

"This is an important book for any teacher looking for ideas about how to prevent male violence. Denny has devoted his life's work to just that goal and he writes both passionately and compassionately about it."

-SAM WEINTRAUB, Ph.D., Professor Emeritus,
Graduate School of Education, SUNY at Buffalo.
Editor of *The Annual Summary of Investigations Relating to Reading.*

"Todd Denny has spent the past two decades developing engaging techniques to inspire young men to become allies in the struggle against male violence. He has a rare gift for enabling students to examine the difficult and critical issues of bullying, sexual harassment and sexual assault."

-Washington State Senate Majority Leader LISA BROWN

"Denny's innovative use of music to educate students about male violence creates excitement, insight and change that are sustained long after the conclusion of his workshops. I highly recommend Todd's curriculum to secondary schools."

-FRED SCHRUMPF, Principal, Havermale High School,
Spokane Public Schools, WA.
Author of *Peer Mediation: Conflict Resolution in Schools.*

"Denny's book is a rare find; he clearly explains how addressing male violence in gender-neutral terms is part of our failure to prevent sexual assault and abuse."

-THERESA SCHINZEL, M.A., Sexual Assault & Harm Prevention,
Department of Justice Grant Manager, Gonzaga University

"I have worked with Todd Denny in California public schools, where he proved to be an effective and engaging change agent. He left the students begging for more."

-CHARLES PRICKETT, J.D., Ph. D.
District Compliance Officer, Santa Rosa Junior College, CA.

Table of Contents

This publication is designed to provide accurate and authoritative information in regard to the subject matter covered. It is sold with the understanding that the publisher is not engaged in rendering legal, accounting or other professional service. If legal advice or other expert assistance is required, the services of a competent professional should be sought.

Fictitious names of individuals and institutions have been used in this book wherever the author thought confidentiality was required.

1 Men - Violence Prevention
2 Women -Violence Against
3 Women - Crimes Against
4 Sex Crimes
5 Youth Violence Prevention

1 Title: Unexpected Allies: Men who Stop Rape

Book Design by Debi Bodett
Cover Photo by Nathan Jones
Order this book online at www.trafford.com/07-0163
or email orders@trafford.com
Most Trafford titles are also available at major online book retailers.

Note for Librarians: A cataloguing record for this book is available from Library and Archives Canada at www.collectionscanada.ca/amicus/index-e.html

ISBN: 978-1-4251-1700-9

www.trafford.com

North America & international
toll-free: 1 888 232 4444 (USA & Canada)
phone: 250 383 6864
fax: 250 383 6804
email: info@trafford.com

The United Kingdom & Europe
phone: +44 (0)1865 722 113
local rate: 0845 230 9601
facsimile: +44 (0)1865 722 868
email: info.uk@trafford.com

10 9 8 7 6 5 4

Introduction

What would inspire a man to devote his life to stopping rape and domestic violence? Traditionally these activities have been considered women's issues exclusively; and men often don't regard violence against women as a problem if their own behavior is nonabusive. Shouldn't men stick to issues that relate exclusively to men? These are reasonable questions that deserve forthright answers.

I discovered my life's path in 1984 during my senior year at The Evergreen State College (TESC). I was enrolled in a year-long interdisciplinary program entitled Ceremonies in Prefigurative Cultures. It was team-taught by three Native American faculty including David Whitener, the Squaxin Island Tribal Chairman. When David stressed that "You must work with your own people in your own community and use the power of groups as opposed to individuals to affect change," his counsel pierced my heart. I embraced the concept of working for change in my own community and sought an internship in Olympia, Washington.

Looking for a challenge, I found it at Safeplace, a rape-relief and domestic-violence women's shelter in Olympia. Six intensive weeks of victim advocacy training opened my eyes to the power of privilege that I was born with as a white, middle-class, heterosexual male. For the first time I understood that my inherited power came with a responsibility to use it to make a difference in my community and culture. Within a year I was coordinating a children's support group at Safeplace and working closely with many young survivors whom I had previously thought of only as abstract victims of rape and abuse. This experience inspired me to broaden my advocacy work by developing skills to prevent the male violence that had shattered the lives of those children.

An early presentation in a large, rural middle school in western Washington increased my awareness of the need for prevention. At the conclusion of a teen dating violence program, my female co-presenter and I distributed small slips of paper to the over one hundred thirteen-and fourteen-year-old girls and asked them to answer anonymously one question with a Yes or a No, "Have you ever had an unwanted sexual experience?" They silently handed us their confidential answers as they filed out of the auditorium. Thirty-one of them had written "Yes." The heartbreaking stories they had shared during the program (e.g., being sexually harassed daily on a school bus by an aggressive group of boys) provided a wake-up call for me regarding the magnitude of the problem of sexual violence toward children (as well as toward adults.)

Later in my career, after yet another reported sexual assault on the Evergreen State campus, I was asked to facilitate the college's first men's rape-prevention discussion. That experience inspired me to develop an ongoing, Men Stopping Rape (MSR) group for the campus and the community. Extensive conversations and insightful exchanges with members of that group increased my awareness of the opportunities that lay in working with men to reclaim truths about who we really are. I learned that efforts to prevent male violence can be a powerful force for change when we form coalitions for that purpose.

Two critical questions have guided my approach to preventing violence against women: Why do I want to do this work and how can I engage other men in this work? My aspiration is to create a fertile ground for transforming my questions about male violence into opportunities for engaging millions of men as allies in stopping violence against women. To say "millions" of men is correct, because that is the scale of the problem – and that is the number of benevolent men who are readily available and the number it will take to get the job done.

I began to search out, meet, and read the work of other men across the United States who led a small, vital movement. The groundbreaking work of the "Men Stopping Rape" group in Madison, Wisconsin and the "Oakland Men's Project" in the 1980's deeply influenced my approach to the issues of masculinity, sexism, and sexual assault.

Many generous women at Safeplace, The Evergreen State College, and the University of Illinois served as my teachers. My mentors were participants in the first generation of anti-rape activism and the feminist movement of the early 1970s. These intrepid, pioneering women brought the issues of sexual assault and domestic violence to the forefront of American society and created the opportunity for men like me to be involved in both victim advocacy and, more importantly, prevention education. If we are to build upon the splendid, lifesaving work of these women, we must honor their history and sacrifices (including death) and extend their concept of social justice through principled alliances with men at the forefront of prevention.

Through my alliance with colleagues at Safeplace, I co-created a series of cross-gender rape prevention workshops at TESC (1984-1988). Later as a graduate student in social work at the University of

Illinois (1988-91), I worked in the Office of the Dean of Students. Upon my arrival, my boss and mentor Mary Ellen O'Shaughnessey, the Assistant Dean of Students, challenged me by saying, "Todd, you're going to be the visible man working against rape on this campus." She gave me the opportunity I needed to work with thousands of men in sustained male violence prevention (MVP) programs. I become a lead trainer and facilitator for the Campus Acquaintance Rape Education (CARE) program – a brilliantly designed education model that exemplified the best in rape prevention training at the time.

I spent my next three years working with men on a campus with the largest university fraternity system in the world (57 houses) as well as with male athletes, and men in residence-life programs. I also worked with community high school boys; team-taught an academic course on acquaintance rape education for peer educators; and created and facilitated an evolving Men Stopping Rape group on the Illinois campus. I became convinced that significant personal changes occur principally when men are immersed in long-term efforts in prevention education. I also learned that cultural myths perpetuate a view of men as stoic and non-caring. A more complete truth about men is much fuller and promising.

Programs that I co-developed and facilitated were featured in the award-winning Public Broadcasting Service documentary, "Date Rape: A Different Set of Rules" (1991). The programs continue to this day.

An overview of the challenges. The MVP movement in the United States remains a small but potentially powerful entity. I strive to build upon the wonderful heritage of the thousands of advocates and educators in the battered-women's and rape-crisis centers across our nation through the young men whom I teach and mentor. Much of my time is spent developing new approaches to involve men in ongoing prevention programs.

Men may appear to be aloof or uninterested about violence prevention, especially when they have not considered the unique and life-transforming possibilities inherent in their involvement as allies with women in the movement. However, their apparent disinterest disappears with education. Some men are simply unaware of or give little thought to the issues of sexual violence and abuse. Although men are earnestly involved in working for social justice in political, social, and environmental arenas, they can find it difficult to acknowledge and increase their awareness of male violence. Accepting responsibility for rape and domestic violence is a daunting, personal challenge and a terrifying proposition for men to embrace. It is easy to ignore this problem knowing that someone else (women) will do the work that men need to do.

The vast majority of those who commit rape, domestic violence, and abuse in our culture are males, age thirteen through twenty-nine and nearly one-third of American women (31 percent) report being physically or sexually abused by a husband or boyfriend at some point in their lives (Collins, K.S., Schoen, C. & Joseph, S., 1999, p.8). To the extent that we fail to acknowledge, examine and remedy these glaring truths, we remain asleep to our current plight and the opportunities for massive social change. Until the cultural taboo of addressing male responsibility for rape is broken, little progress will be made to reduce the pandemic levels of male violence.

It is also quite clear to me that young men are often merely stereotyped as "the problem" and approached poorly – even by educators who wish to stop violence against women. We must counter the perception that men are exclusively perpetrators and start seeing them as major contributors to the cure. Unconscious stereotypes of men can operate as barriers to our prevention work. Millions of men neither condone nor engage in violence against women. As natural allies they can become a vital part of the solution to break the cycle of violence that includes sexual assault, domestic violence, and abuse. Men are interested in learning how to live without violence and in broadening their influence when offered the opportunity to do so.

Childhood influences. If everyone can cultivate the seeds of compassion and peace within themselves, then how do things go wrong? Familial and cultural influences can transform innocent boys into abusive men, who then repeat their childhood abuse with their own children in a cycle of violence that is perpetuated in succeeding generations. Impressionable young boys (and girls) mirror their environments, both good and bad.

The roots of why I'm involved with MVP programs can be traced to my childhood in a stable and caring home. But the violence I witnessed and experienced outside my home left its mark on me. In my large, culturally diverse middle school in Illinois, an incident occurred that may provide additional insight into why I'm involved in this work.

While students were jostling in the halls between classes, I noticed an older boy bullying a younger one. He shoved his head into a drinking fountain and shattered a front tooth. The bully laughed gleefully at his prank, while the smaller boy pulled back in surprise and pain with blood running down his face onto his shirt. A whirlwind of emotions churned within me: astonishment, anger, sadness and powerlessness. I felt rage for the actions of the thug and a tug of compassion for the suffering boy – yet I stood paralyzed. How could I help without using violence and possibly become his next target? What can one do when confronted with unjust use of force, other than make another aggressive response? This experience was an early motivation for my involvement with men's violence prevention and fostered nonviolent intervention as a principal learning goal in my workshops.

My home environment, the drinking fountain experience, a wise male teacher in college, and my Safeplace internship were significant influences on my career.

I know we can significantly reduce rape, abuse, and other forms of male violence by creating opportunities for boys and men to participate in imaginatively-designed education programs. The young men who I mentor and teach harbor latent altruistic qualities that are ready to be nurtured. Since men are so often the problem, they simply have to be a part of the solution if we want to stop violence against women.

Why I am writing this book. This book is a "took kit" for violence prevention educators who work with young men (and women), are willing to examine the roots of male violence in our culture and are committed to taking the necessary steps to initiate and sustain successful programs. I have several audiences in mind, including middle and high school teachers and college staff, fraternity leaders, coaches, community sexual assault/domestic violence educators, women's center and criminal justice system personnel.

Is the problem of men who commit rape and domestic violence so ingrained and widespread in our culture as to be unsolvable? No. Should we abandon the possibility of a multitude of men taking the lead to stop this violence? We should not. Should we continue to work with women to help prevent their victimization? Of course! Can we create and support programs in which young men commit themselves to work to stop this violence? Yes. There are far better models and approaches to these issues than those most educators now use. Male violence prevention holds a promise that is both large and unfulfilled in our society.

Male violence against women is vastly under-reported (some estimate the reports to be less than 10 percent of its actual occurrence). Because it is largely kept out of societal sight, it is kept out of our minds. The dollar costs are staggering. Overall, rape has the highest annual victim costs at $127 billion per year (excluding child sex abuse), followed by assault at $93 billion, murder at $61 billion, and child abuse at $56 billion (Miller, Cohen & Wiersma, 1996, p.1). An improvement of a few percentage points would result in billions of savings.

Immeasurably more important, of course, are the deaths and shattered lives that would be averted. How many families would remain intact? How many women might keep or regain their trust in men? How many young men would not have to appear in our courts or populate our prisons? How many men could live their lives beyond narrow gender role expectations? How many might lead lives non-abusive to women and influence the spread of such qualities to other men?

A sobering statistic: sixty-one percent of all female rape survivors are victimized during their preteen and teenage years (American Academy of Pediatrics, 1994). Clearly, teachers of preteens should address this issue; yet in practice, honest discussion of sexual violence is taboo in many high schools and almost nonexistent in middle school curricula.

On the rare occasions when rape is discussed in our schools, its historical focus is almost exclusively on educating young women (the victims) – overlooking the young men who are overwhelmingly the perpetrators (Greenfield, 1997, p.10). Why is rape/violence discussed in abstract and gender-neutral terms instead of calling it what it is: men raping women and men abusing women? It indicates the difficulty of acknowledging that "regular guys" commit the vast majority of sexual and domestic violence in our culture. Some educators apparently find it easier (personally or politically) to focus on reducing women's risk than to address the source of the problem. Our dominant culture's power elite is comprised primarily of white, heterosexual men who rarely acknowledge much less examine the issues of sexism, masculinity and violence against women. It is less threatening for men to support advocacy for female victims (of male violence) than to look honestly within themselves to face the values that beget rape and abuse. Stories about female victims of abuse are in the daily news. Only rarely do we hear or read about the acquaintances, boyfriends, and husbands who perpetrated these crimes. Even less frequently do we examine and discuss the beliefs that condone, encourage and legitimize men's violence against women.

Boys start learning what it is to "be a man" at a young age, most often from their fathers or surrogate fathers. They commonly learn that expressions of aggression are acceptable, expected, and appropriate for men. They are taught to suppress their feelings of openness and compassion, and are reminded that such qualities are both effeminate and shameful. They develop a fear of expressing themselves, a fear that straightjackets them within an identity of cultural machismo. Steve, a high school junior from Urbana, Illinois, candidly framed a part of the problem: "I'm always putting up a front and not letting my feelings show." Encouragingly, most men are uncomfortable with what they have been taught about being a man, including their inability to express themselves emotionally and their own sexist behaviors (Berkowitz, 2003).

Boys also face early, relentless pressure to separate from their parents. Men in our society rarely model or teach boy's heart-based attitudes and actions; instead they inculcate values of being independent and tough. Only a small group of men in our society are aware of the sources of their impulses and understand the potentially destructive consequences of their violent actions.

Media violence is a concern. Research findings on how individual, environmental and content factors moderate the effects of exposure to media violence are unclear. Although limited in scope and depth, studies do provide clues to potential avenues for prevention efforts. For example, preliminary data point to the potentially vital role of parents in supervising their children's exposure to violent media and in helping them to interpret it (Nathanson, 1999).

That media contribute to male violence is a partial truth. Certainly the media influence young psyches, but their sway is secondary to the impact of abusive men (and women) during a child's formative years. Many men convicted of crimes, including sexual assault and battery, reveal the abuse they received as children, illuminating how their adult lives have perpetuated the cycle of violence. Rape and domestic violence are not innate male qualities; they are learned behaviors and they can be unlearned.

One in four women will be a victim of an attempted or completed sexual assault during her lifetime. Her life will be dramatically changed, usually by someone she trusted: a classmate, acquaintance, friend, family member, or husband (Warshaw, 1994). Unknown predators are *not* the assailants of most rape victims. Most women are raped by someone they know (Warshaw, 1994). Millions of boys and men are also survivors of sexual assault; they, too, have usually been assaulted by men among their families, close relations or acquaintances (Snyder, 2000).

Men as well as women can be misled and confused about gender violence, when they accept generations-old misinformation about the nature and the consequences of unwarranted male force. By recasting men as the solution to the problem, we counteract untenable assumptions about male violence and chart a new path for action and change. Over time we can transform men's images from being associated only with the stigma (and truth) of being perpetrators to becoming leaders in stopping sexual violence and abuse. By concentrating on what is inherently good in men and building on it we help transform them and our culture.

It is extremely important to create "safe spaces" where men can examine their life histories and personalize their experiences without fear of finger-pointing. My goal is to balance the necessary feeling of safety with creating an awareness and acceptance of personal responsibility for the vast majority of violence. Because young men are so aware of and sensitive to how their peers regard them, I work to create a climate wherein the nonabusive male majority can negate the abusive attitudes and behavior of a minority of their peers.

In my workshops I define sexual assault and domestic violence prevention as issues of male leadership. I use the chronology of men's life experiences as a nonthreatening way to examine some of the harmful and abusive ways that men learn to be male. During our discussions, I enable men to move from memories of their childhood to their young adulthood, always with an attitude of positive expectancy. This enables men to understand the connections between masculinity, antifemale beliefs and behaviors, with the problems of male violence against women. My approach represents a sharp departure from the historical practice of focusing narrowly on the outcomes of male violence and can inspire men's earnest involvement in redefining themselves as MVP leaders. I devote several chapters to the details of my approach.

Music and male violence prevention education. I engage young men and women within unique music programs that coalesce nicely with my overall approach to VP (see Chapter 3). The music of popular culture is an educational vehicle that is almost irresistible to youth. Furthermore, music can attract men who normally would not be interested or involved in male violence prevention – e.g., athletes, musicians, incarcerated juveniles, and boys awash in the commodified and marketed "gang member" mentality. They are the very men we desperately seek to engage! It is both easy and misguided to dismiss the hip-hop music of youth culture simply because it fails to fit a particular aesthetic notion of beauty. Granted, some popular music (including rock and country) features lyrics that glorify abusive ideas of masculinity and unacceptable views of women. But when we work with youth in their own language and culture, we can transform misogynistic lyrics into positive messages that can change the student musicians and their listening peers.

I am often astonished by the depth of students' immersion in their creative work – and by what I learn from them when I use music to reach my educational goals. Initially our MVP music project attracted a core of twenty young men from area high schools, colleges, and the community – who volunteered over the course of three years to speak out, rap, and sing against racism, sexism, homophobia, and sexual assault. Their lives were fundamentally changed by their long-term involvement in an innovative, community-based project that gave them an opportunity to examine and express their own beliefs about male violence. Our music curriculum does not regard youth as mere consumers of educational media created by adults; rather it helps them engage in meaningful social interactions and personal change through the process of their creating poetry and song for themselves and their peers.

Music is so alluring that we have to restrict the number of students who are involved during our week-long, school-residency program. Capitalizing on the music of youth culture to create songs with uplifting and life-affirming messages is an approach to preventing male violence that succeeds when all others have failed.

Our opportunity. I write for and work with educators who are willing to change and adapt their approaches, who can acknowledge that some of their own work has not been fruitful, and desire to examine and drop old prejudices. Educators, like the young men with whom we work, must be willing to think in fresh ways, take risks, and make adjustments based on their experience and reports of best practice about how young men (and women) respond to various educational programs. There are other excellent public health VP models and I believe they could be even more successful if they adapted my approaches to their work.

If you are willing to accept the proposition – or at least to explore the idea – that men are responsible for the vast majority of violence toward women (and men); and that many men are ready and willing to become leaders to reverse this fact, then you already possess two of the tools required for building a life-transforming male violence prevention program. This book moves beyond analysis and discussion of the problem of male violence and shows the reader how to transform boys and men from passive to active participants in violence prevention. I will provide you with ideas and techniques for making empowering behavioral changes in young men regarding violence against women. This book is about results!

ONE

Unexpected Allies

Why should men remain the problem when we can inspire them to become the solution?

ONE HUNDRED DIVISION I FOOTBALL players are crammed into a small auditorium to hear a "lecture" on rape. Having just finished a three-hour practice, they are not overjoyed to be spending free time off the field with me. It's a boisterous, loud, joking, and inattentive group. I begin the workshop amidst the clamor while thinking, "This might be a rough session." My first exercise starts without the attention of many; unexpectedly John, a huge senior offensive lineman, rises and startles the entire group by yelling, "Everyone shut up and listen. This is important! I know – my girlfriend was raped!" An uneasy hush fills the room as the stunned players turn to look at their team leader, who remains standing. Tightened lips reflected John's frustration as he slowly surveys the group, letting his words sink in. He has both silenced the din of chatter and established a dividing line between indifference and knowledge.

John's outburst sparked a highly interactive workshop in which team members shared introspective stories about violence in their lives and in the lives of the women they loved. John provided inspiration that was more powerful than anything a trainer could say or do. Such actions by participants are not unusual in my workshops. Young men repeatedly step up to refocus or reenergize a group.

Unfortunately, we don't create sufficient opportunities for men to take the lead in stopping violence against women. In my workshops, many young men like John take their first positive action toward becoming an ally in stopping rape. When I create opportunities for them, men step up: high-school boys, fraternity presidents, athletes, formerly incarcerated youth and countless others.

Marcus, a junior in a small Alabama high-school, expressed his conviction during an MVP workshop to a group of forty of his peers: "We can stand up for our own beliefs about rape when dealing with other men." As facilitators we must examine our own assumptions about men before we can help them change their lives. It is easy to stereotype the football players in ways that prevent them from becoming united in rape prevention. Through introspection and insightful exchange, we can change both our unfounded assumptions about men and our ideas about their abilities to positively influence other men.

Stafford confirmed his role as an unexpected ally in an Illinois university co-ed workshop, when he described his intervention in a likely rape situation:

> "When I was in high school, I was at a 'kegger' party where alcohol was flowing freely. I noticed a girl who was quite drunk being pulled by a guy toward an isolated room in the back of the house. He had targeted and separated her from the group and was clearly taking advantage of her condition. To their surprise I quickly stepped between them

> and confronted him with, 'What do you think your doing?' He menacingly retorted with, 'F off.'
>
> "The young woman slurred, 'Tell him to leave me alone.' Standing face-to-face (to the antagonist) I said, 'Back off, man' and held my ground, blocking his way. He feigned hitting me – but I didn't flinch. Seeing that I meant business he looked perplexed and uneasy. After a few tense moments he released the girl's arm, muttered further obscenities and walked away. I returned to the party with the girl, found one of her friends, explained the situation and she gave her a ride home."

After recounting his intervention Stafford sat down to the applause of his peers.

We must discard ineffective approaches such as preaching at men and develop new keys to their involvement. One such key is to dismiss our one-shot treatments. The effect of a single MVP presentation pales in comparison to the impact that a long-term program can have on changing male beliefs and behaviors. Engaging men in ongoing MVP programs affords them the opportunity to reflect on how their experiences while growing up male may have contributed to violence against women and how they can be part of a solution.

That is a start. But how can we keep men interested, involved, and inspired over the course of several years or a lifetime? First, teachers and mentors must change their expectations of men. Historically, women have taken almost all the risks and done the majority of the work, educating both women and men on issues of sexual assault and domestic violence. I would not be doing this work if it were not for the training and support of my Safeplace mentors.

My experience suggests that male mentors have an advantage over women in changing men's beliefs regarding sexual aggression. Men are also more successful in keeping other men involved in ongoing efforts, just as women are more effective than men in educating and helping women who have survived sexual assault and domestic violence.

At the end of a successful workshop with a university fraternity in Tacoma, Washington, Ben, its president, pulled me aside as I prepared to leave: "I'm looking for a job this summer, do you have any opportunities for me to work with you?" If I had stereotyped Ben as an insensitive frat guy, I would have missed this opportunity to collaborate. The subsequent involvement of Ben's fraternity is an example of success that I incorporate in my MVP workshops; it was featured internationally on a European television program that examined rape in America.

I discovered a seemingly unlikely ally during a rap music festival. I was looking for talent for our MVP music project and had heard glowing reports of a local rapper. I approached Terrance, who had been out of prison for less then a year after a court had given him a juvenile "life" sentence for gang-related activities. I explained my project and asked, "What do you think of violence against women?" Looking me directly in the eyes he quickly replied, "I don't do it." Within a year Terrance evolved into the star of our MVP music project, touring western America performing for and educating thousands of students. (For details about how to use music in a male violence-prevention program, see "It's About You, Man" in Chapter 3).

A recurring lesson in my workshops has been the need to expand the view we have of men. Being a "real man" transcends racial, ethnic, and socioeconomic lines and too often celebrates and reinforces aggressive, controlling behaviors that underpin male violence. I believe that the violent persona of being a "real man" conflicts with many men's desire to develop their true selves. In my programs participants share their life stories of being caring and nonabusive men, who want to lead lives free of violence. Indeed, they are the new "real men."

Nobody wants others to point to their past mistakes since everyone has committed errors in judgment. As educators we must move beyond blame. By seeing more in young men than they may see in themselves, we will contribute to their development as leaders in rape prevention. I live my life with an attitude of positive expectancy. Men respond to the expectations I have of them to be respectful, honest and helpful. I work as if men will both understand and respond to my expectations. Certainly there have been and will be disappointments. But if I am going to err, it is going to be on the positive side.

I am not a lone voice crying out in the wilderness. I heard Mike Krzyzewski, Duke University's splendid basketball coach speak positively about his approach to young male athletes. He said,

> "Kids are great now, and they were great twenty years ago. They come from different cultures, but if we continue to try to teach these kids from the culture we know best (or the only one we want to know), we'll always think of them as being hard to coach. If we try to adapt to the culture they're in and still teach principles of honesty, trust, togetherness and teamwork, we'll have a chance."

Krzyzewski concluded by saying, "And you know what? You might just find the perfect blending of two cultures, which is what I think people are all about."

Until men are helped to examine and change their values, they behave much like the hypermasculine men they knew in their childhood homes, observed in their neighborhoods, participated with in sports and saw on television. We can help men unlearn harmful behaviors and replace them with the positive attributes they need to become leaders. Can we change fifteen to twenty years of male socialization in a single workshop? Probably not. Can we engage men in ongoing discussions about rape and abuse that inspire them to prevent violence against women? Absolutely!

Prevention efforts that are positive in tone assist men who are seeking ways to express their true feelings. Ryan, a fraternity member at a Boston college, posed insightful questions during a coed IFC/ Pan-Hellenic workshop,

- "What do women want in a relationship?
- What would make it easier for us to communicate with them?
- What would they prefer?"

The effect of his questions was profound. The entire energy of the room was transfixed on a man intent on creating a greater degree of mutual understanding. Our role is to enable men to change their ideas about themselves while we change our own perceptions of them. It is a challenging task because men's desires to express their true selves honestly often conflict with social pressure to be "one of the guys." A sexual harassment workshop I facilitated for a community group illustrates this point. After a participant brusquely commented, "Screw the feelings (of men); we need to look at their actions. Andy, a younger male replied, "I disagree, I'm tired of being told to hide my feelings, I've heard that since I was a boy." By offering men the opportunity to reexamine the acculturation that led to their views of "masculinity" they are prepared to develop intervention skills to prevent abuse against women.

A poignant intervention was shared by my colleague David Hellstrom, during a peer-educator workshop.

> It was New Year's Eve in a downtown hotel that had several bands in its ballrooms. It was packed, many were drinking heavily and by the end of the evening the place was filled with over-served people.
>
> I was in a crowded men's restroom waiting for my "turn" when the entrance door opened and in walked, or I should say stumbled, a young woman. She announced very drunkenly that "Our line's way too long in the women's bathroom" and that she "couldn't wait." She went into an open stall.
>
> Most of the men in the room were surprised and found it to be humorous. The mood quickly turned sour when a guy pushed open the woman's stall door. She yelled, "Let me get my pants on you BLANK!" Blocking her exit, he announced that she wasn't leaving because she "owed the guys something" for letting her use their bathroom. Soon several men joined him, holding her "captive" in the stall.
>
> This was turning into an ugly situation. The mood had turned from funny to predatory, and I didn't think they were going to let her out. So, I squeezed through the group until I could grab her by the arm and trying to keep things

light I said, "Darling, you can't come in here – it's not our fault that you ladies take so long to pee."

I then quickly pulled her through the group and out of the restroom. Some men gave me an incredulous look that said, "Why are you wrecking this?" The intoxicated woman swore at me the whole time – but I firmly held her until we were safely in the hallway.

I have no doubt that a rape, or at least some form of sexual assault was unfolding in that men's room. Guys who had no thoughts of violence when they entered the room, and who would not have considered themselves to be potential rapists, got caught up in a "mob mentality." They were on the verge of committing gang rape.

Things can happen quickly. Even "good guys" who would have not participated might have allowed it to happen. Alcohol abuse by men and women in social settings distorts reality, clouds and erodes good judgment and can contribute to sexual violence.

I'll never forget it.

Lorenzo, a graduate student and peer educator at a Los Angeles community college, shared his dramatic intervention experience in a coed workshop:

"When I was only nine, I was at home with my sister. My parents were out for the night. I heard my sister cry for help

> when she was being sexually assaulted by two male 'friends' in our living room. I reacted instinctively in spite of the danger, grabbed a baseball bat and bolted out of my bedroom and attacked the men who were restraining my sister on the couch. Swinging desperately I somehow managed to hit them repeatedly and drove them out of our house. Walking back into our home my sister and I looked at each other in shock and disbelief, while trying to make sense of all that had occurred in a few moments."

Lorenzo was fortunate to have stopped the assault and lived to share his heroic tale. The effect of his disclosure was startling. A long silence ensued after the young men and women heard his story.

Our quest is to change our preconceptions about men as perpetrators of violence and to help them assume their rightful roles as partners in prevention. How will we ever get there? A start would be to work with men with the same compassion and understanding we have for survivors of abuse. In my work as a teacher, I've discovered that approaching men from a different perspective and looking at the situation from their point of view can have a transforming effect. We must also strive to become aware of obstructions that we may be inadvertently creating during our work with students, athletes, fraternity members, and incarcerated youth. I can assure you that it is possible to "get there." I have seen it happen again and again when I approach men in a nonaccusatory, supportive manner. Men are interested in learning how to live fulfilled lives. If we look closely, we might discover several things in a man: the boy who stopped a bully from hurting a weaker child and the mentor, volunteer or big brother.

Three fundamental tenets underlie this book and, I believe, any successful program that addresses male violence.

1. The first tenet unmasks the pernicious myth that men do not want to change their beliefs about violence against women. Hundreds of workshops and training sessions with thousands of men have convinced me that finding men to mentor is not difficult. Our task is to create ways to touch their inner beings – their innate benevolence and life experiences – in order to inspire them to help prevent sexual violence. Many men have girlfriends, sisters, and mothers who have survived sexual assault. This anonymous story from Brian, a freshman from a Big Ten university, describes that reality:

   > "When I was about four years old a man broke into my house. He wanted to rape my mother but she fought him off. He was eventually arrested. I felt confused, afraid and upset after the assault and wanted him to be in jail forever."

   Men have mothers, daughters, and female friends who have been physically or psychologically brutalized in ways other than rape. Talk with a man at length and eventually you will discover an incident of gender-based violence that permanently marked his life or the life of someone he cares about. Examining such experiences has the latent power to forever change men's beliefs about interpersonal violence. Sharing one's own and hearing others' experiences about the consequences of abuse heighten men's awareness. When men understand the underpinning familial and cultural influences of male violence, they can then realize their own potential for preventing it.

Men with high visibility are working to reduce sexism and violence against women. Examples include Kenny Smith, the popular television basketball analyst and former NBA star, who said "No" to Playboy magazine when it nominated him for its All-American team, a pseudo sports award designed to boost magazine sales with male sports fans. So did Rasheed Wallace of the NBA Detroit Pistons and Duke University's head basketball coach Mike Krzyzewski.

Lorenzo Romar, the highly successful University of Washington basketball coach, took a public stand against domestic violence. Recounting how it personally influenced his home life as a child he stated frankly that, "You feel helpless." Romar describes his mentoring of high-profile players, "I talk to them about seeing it, going through it (because) as much as you despise it, you can end up doing the same thing yourself." He accepts no excuses for male abuse such as, "She just wouldn't listen" or "I had to get her attention" (Paynter, 2004, p.F6).

2. My second tenet is that men who are involved in ongoing programs, such as men's stopping rape groups and peer-education training, are the ones most likely to be changed. No one unlearns fifteen to twenty years of hurtful attributes about masculinity after a single program. It's a sustained process over time. How does one dismantle the ideological framework and acceptance of patriarchy and male abuse? By methodically

examining, critiquing, and reasoning with men about the inherent limitations and harm such ideologies have for women as well as men. Traditional approaches to MVP require young men to attend a single lecture. Such presentations are often facilitated solely by women, who do the majority of work as both victim advocates and educators. But such programs – even those facilitated by men – rarely inspire male involvement. Involved men can both reduce the pressure felt by thousands of women who carry most of the burden as antiviolence educators and make VP programs more effective, too. Men Can Stop Rape (2007), a Washington D.C. organization engages high school boys with their exemplary, sixteen-week "Men of Strength Clubs."

Men cannot be reached by telling them to "Do this" or "Stop doing that." Preaching is rarely effective and lectures are lethal for any effort to engage men in life-transforming programs. MVP educators must be innovatively proactive. Hoping for male involvement and merely waiting for it to occur has become the collective failure of the movement. I invite you to transform your hope into action:

- What will you do when you are finished reading this chapter?

- Will you take concrete steps to enhance your prevention work?

- Will you organize a series of meetings on your campus or in your community? (See Chapter 8.)

Keeping men engaged and motivated in ongoing programs is a continual challenge for aspiring MVP group leaders. MVP groups and awareness campaigns can begin optimistically and fade into obscurity. The demise of the previously-mentioned "Men Stopping Rape" group in Madison, Wisconsin and "The Oakland Men's Project" are two disappointing examples. Convening men merely for the purpose of attending a lecture or two, regardless of how sterling the intention, won't get the job done. At the conclusion of my MVP workshops men often share stories about previous mandatory "rape lectures" that left them uninspired, bored, targeted, or worse.

Although group discussions conducted to raise consciousness are an important first step, they will not ensure sustainability. Once you have created awareness, it must be followed by action; otherwise the program will remain at the intellectual level of just talk. Interactive workshops, peer education, theater, music, and protests create momentum and help promote continuing male involvement. The more time and energy that men devote to this process, the more likely they are to change the way they live their daily lives, and use their ability to influence other men in positive ways. Men engaged in ongoing prevention programs can recreate themselves and change their surrounding culture of male power, privilege, and injustice. We must not lose sight of young men's futures as teachers, coaches, jurors, and law enforcement officers. Most importantly, they will become fathers who can mentor boys and other men in life-affirming ways.

An example of a man stepping up occurred several years ago when I led a dating-violence workshop for high school students. We had examined the cycle of violence, the seeds sown, and the harmful behavior learned within homes characterized by anger and abuse (see Chapter 2). At the program's end, Nick, an eighteen-year-old program participant, spoke with me privately. He disclosed that he came from an abusive home where his dad was violent with him and his siblings. He motioned to his girlfriend across the room and said that he was now raising a child of his own. He insightfully asked, "What can I do to make sure I'm not abusive to my child?" I was touched by Nick's honesty and felt honored to have a serious conversation with another man committed to stopping the cycle of violence. Nick's awareness had been raised and he sought further action, thereby fulfilling my first two tenets.

3. My third tenet is that men, simply because of their male presence, stature, language and male culture, can influence other men more easily than can women. A case in point: imagine a group of young men attending a mandatory rape-education workshop on campus. Who do you think would have the greater influence on this group: a competent, female educator or a collegiate football player speaking candidly about men's responsibility for stopping rape? In all likelihood it would be the athlete. Group dynamics change when women facilitate MVP programs – and not always for the better. Credible male facilitators can quickly extinguish patronizing, defensive and sexist reactions of male participants. We can help young men change their deeply held beliefs by not blaming them for espousing misinformation and helping them develop a new perspective. This approach can promote broad reflection and insightful exchange. Male presenters who unabashedly model behaviors that refute male dominance have a considerable positive impact on other males.

To the extent that we are unaware of our own assumptions about men, to that extent we are controlled by our ignorance. It has taken me a long time to unlearn many of my assumptions and beliefs about men's possibilities as allies and mentors; and I continue to monitor myself during my programs. Assumptions in and of themselves are common and sometimes useful. After two decades of work with young men and women, I have learned to be careful about preconceptions I may form based on superficial phenomena such as participants' appearances. Read the following statements made by students in my rape prevention workshops:

> "Sexual assault does not take away women's power."
>
> "Men face much more pressure to be accepted by other men than women do."
>
> "When is a woman's role in sexual aggression recognized? Did she 'ask' for it? Was she promiscuous?"

Strong statements indeed! What do you think you know after reading them? You may have formed an impression about the people who wrote them. Now read a second set of statements made by another group of workshop participants:

> "Feel comfortable about being open and assertive, telling me what you want and don't want, both sexually and emotionally."

"Don't be afraid to communicate what you are expecting in any dating situation. No offense will be taken and respect will be given."

"I think all women should carry a gun."

Have you made assumptions about the two groups after reading their statements? What can we reasonably assume about the people in either group?

The first thing you should know is that the anonymous statements in the first group were written by women – and, yes, the second group's statements were written by men. Be careful about assumptions! Oh, the trouble we get into when we presume to know what women think and what men think! An empowering assumption we can make is that men want to be the allies of women in stopping sexual violence.

As obvious as it may seem, few men have examined the underpinning experiences that contribute to male violence. What are the major influences that teach boys to be aggressive and abusive? How do boys grow up in a way that normalizes violence and makes it a part of the status quo? How do young men move from childhood innocence to perpetuation of interpersonal violence and sexual assault? My next chapter discusses what is known about issues related to the developmental cycle of male violence.

TWO

The Cards We Were Dealt

The greatest thing a father can do for his children
is to love their mother.

A METAPHORIC WAY TO THINK about violence in our communities and schools is to consider the cards the game of life dealt us. Gender, class, race, sexual orientation, and ability are all significant factors interacting with the violence we experience and perpetuate throughout our lives. Gender is the best predictor of being a perpetrator of sexual assault and abuse, because ninety-nine percent of all rapists are men (Greenfield, 1997, p.2 and p.10). And the greatest chance of becoming a victim of rape or domestic violence lies with being a woman (Warshaw, 1994, p.11). Another card dealt in the hand of life is our family – especially our parents. Brutal parents and, most often abusive fathers, are rarely discussed catalysts for the domestic violence that victimizes so many youth in our society. If you want to find an underpinning influence on the schoolyard bully (read 'boy'), just knock on the door of his house and meet the large-sized version, his dad or surrogate father. We have to face the facts. Not everything faced can be changed

– but nothing can be changed until it is faced. Having a penchant for violence is not an abstract personality characteristic that occurs randomly. Violence is a learned behavior – and thankfully it can be unlearned.

In his powerful book, *Finding Freedom: Writings from Death Row*, Jarvis Masters inquired about the scars that covered the bodies of his friends in San Quentin Prison (Masters, 1997, p.68-71). Fellow inmate John recalled,

> "The day that I got used to getting beaten by my father and by the counselors (surrogate fathers) in all those group homes was the day I knew nothing would ever hurt me again."
>
> "The histories of all of us in San Quentin were so similar it was if we had the same parents. I doubt if any of them (inmates) would have used the word 'abuse' to describe their childhood."

John said that his father had "loved him enough" to teach him when he was only five years old to fight. He learned from the beatings that he received. David and Pete recounted similar childhood experiences. Their stories said much about how they came to be in one of the worst prisons in the country.

How do we as a society view these prisoners, many of whom are survivors of domestic violence? Some think they were "born that way." A revealing comment was made during a legislative hearing that I attended in Olympia, Washington. The Director of Corrections, while pleading his case for more prison cells, argued that "Many of these men are criminal by nature." (I suspect he changed his mind when, sadly and ironically, his own son was convicted of rape a year after the hearing.)

The Director's negative view about the nature of men does not square with my experience with a juvenile inmate from the streets of Seattle. Freddy was unpredictably violent and had earned fear and respect from his fellow prisoners. I reviewed his case file and learned that Freddy, like many of the other incarcerated boys, was from an abusive family. He was living on his own by the time he was fourteen. To return to our metaphor, Freddy was not dealt a good hand. I witnessed him purposely getting tear-gassed and then body-slammed to the floor by a prison guard during a tense standoff. After the altercation, while in excruciating pain with a flushed red face and eyes streaming with tears, he justified his actions by boasting; "I just wanted to see what it was like to get gassed." I befriended Freddy and occasionally spent time talking with him in his cell. No one on the 'outside' called, wrote, or cared for him. A victim of domestic violence, this sixteen-year-old felon was a thoughtful, afraid, and traumatized young man.

Fears spawned early in life lie at the heart of much of the violence in our culture's youth. No innate need for aggression causes male violence – but fear often precedes and is the companion of such violence. Youth who live in fear in their homes, schools and communities are more inclined to perpetuate violence than are those who live in emotionally secure environments. A boy is much more likely to respond to adversity with violence if he lives his life looking over his shoulder in anticipation of it. Nonabusive men almost always have not lived in fear. There are, of course, pathological cases of violence that do not grow out of fear – but in the vast majority of young men, there are strong connections between fear, anger and violence. An elementary school teacher explained the early precursors of violence that she found in her violent young students "The violent kids are the ones who come from homes filled with anger. They're angry about what goes on in their homes. They're already angry when they arrive at the schoolhouse door."

The cards we are dealt include the opportunities and constraints that we receive in life. Contrast an African-American child growing up in the notorious Cabrini Green project of Chicago with a Euro-American kid who lives a few miles away in Oak Park, Illinois; or a black child from East St. Louis with a white one from an affluent suburb of western St. Louis. In America we want to believe that our youth have equal opportunities, but we know it is not true. In his insightful and disturbing book Savage Inequalities, Jonathon Kozol methodically lays out the vastly different social, economic, and educational opportunities that are inherent in social class, race, and the demographics of our nation (Kozol, 1991, pp 149-159).

People who come from stable, loving, and caring families often mirror their early experiences in their current lives. Children play the game of life with the cards they were dealt. Nevertheless, we must address an unavoidable truth: overwhelmingly boys and men commit the violence in our nation.

Let's pause for a bit of self reflection:

- How did your family handle conflict, be it parent-child, child-child or parent-parent?

- What did you learn about conflict from your parent(s)?

- How did you learn to respond to conflict when it arose in your family?

My dad was raised in urban Detroit in a second-generation Irish-German Catholic household, while my mom, born of first-generation Lithuanian parents, was reared in rural Dearborn, Michigan. In my father's family, women were expected to bring in income; in my mother's family, women were to be homemakers. Understandably my parents had differences of opinion about religion and work, and there were conflicts about economic issues, too. But in our home these issues as well as other value and cultural differences were settled by conversations, arguments, accommodation and negotiation. There was neither psychological brutality nor physical fighting. Our family disagreements commonly resulted in building relationships and/or agreeing to disagree. Conflict was neither framed nor resolved by shame, humiliation or violence. (Violence is more likely to occur where there is guilt or shame.) In my family we learned that although conflict was a normal part of life it didn't include violence. We got angry, disagreed, negotiated and accommodated. Our resolutions weren't perfect, but they were achieved without psychological or physical violence.

Conflicts are not inherently bad; they are part of our everyday lives and can be empowering learning experiences and teachable moments in our work with young men. All families have their conflicts; it's the quality of the process of resolution that counts. My next story reveals how violence can erupt over seemingly trivial matters in some homes.

Rodney, a Seattle middle school student, had been picked up by the police at home. Because it was already October and he was an eighth grader not enrolled in school, Rodney was adjudged to be truant. Fred, a social worker and close friend of mine was called in to intervene. He asked Rodney, "What happened?" Rodney related that his mom and her boyfriend, his sister, and he were having lunch together when, "All hell broke loose." Lunch was Tater Tots and his job was to divide equal amounts of the bag among them. "An argument broke out between me and my mom's boyfriend over the food shares and we got fighting." Someone called 911, the boyfriend was arrested, and Rodney was taken to the Truancy Center.

When Rodney was asked, "Were those Tater Tots worth fighting over?" he quickly responded, "At our house we fight over everything!" The odds were that once enrolled in school (whenever he attended), Rodney would fight over 'everything' there as well. In his home he learned to resolve conflict through violence.

Many violent boys are themselves traumatized survivors of sexual abuse and domestic violence (Greenfield, 1997, p.23). Without intervention, their future will be a rerun of the present – continuing what musician/poet Gil Scott-Heron (1975) in his prophetic lyrics called *"Winter in America."* Parents pass the seeds of violence to their children, as their parents did to them, from generation to generation. When we understand the roots of violence, we learn to bring compassion to our work with violent boys because we know that many are likely victims caught in the cycle of violence. Compassion is an important first step – but we must couple it with remedy.

Addressing and accepting our responsibility as men for the overwhelming amount of violence that men cause is a pivotal aspect of remedy. Violent offenders typically are males, ages fourteen to twenty-nine; their rap sheets typically include battery, assault, and sexual violence (Greenfeld, 1997). Until we men accept the facts about violent male offenders, little will change. I and other authors and educators, such as John Stoltenberg (1990, p.24) have long argued that continuing to address violence in gender-neutral terms is at the heart of our failure to prevent violence and provide remedy.

We live in a society that victimizes millions of women annually and must take action to improve that culture. If men become aware that their silence and inaction toward violence against women may be seen as condoning that violence, their sense of responsibility increases. It is equally important to remember that we also live in a culture where most men are *not* violent. Furthermore, although most male violence perpetrators were themselves abused, a majority of these men do *not* continue the cycle of violence.

In 1984, when I began volunteering in my community at Safeplace, I occasionally felt uneasy during my training. I was one of four men, working among twenty women in a program designed to prepare us to become domestic violence/sexual assault advocates. Like many men, I found it difficult to find the courage to accept the facts of male violence in our culture.

After the first two weeks of our advocacy training at Safeplace, two men dropped out without a word. Perhaps they, too, felt defensive and thought they had been judged unfairly as males. When male conditioning kicks in, we have to restrain ourselves against reacting with harsh words and emotions to salve our feelings. We also tend to dismiss the personal relevance of the situation. I once heard John Stoltenberg call this defense "Teflon morality," where nothing sticks to men regarding their responsibility for violence. Gradually over the six-week course I grew to see male violence in our culture for what it is and tried harder to be honest with myself. I learned that acceptance is the foundation of change. I also began to understand the power of ongoing involvement in education programs to help men change their engrained beliefs and behaviors.

My understanding of the roots of male violence was influenced further by my advocacy work with victims of domestic and sexual violence, many of whom had been abused by their fathers, surrogate fathers, and boyfriends. Six years of working with children who were survivors of male domestic violence and sexual abuse profoundly increased my awareness. To their stories I have added many others about male abuse that I've heard from female friends.

Acceptance of my responsibility for male violence against women, neither an overnight nor painless process for me, has been foundational in my personal transformation. With that acceptance, I could move beyond my defensiveness and the mere blaming of male perpetrators to my work of creating opportunities for other men to be involved in violence-prevention efforts.

Even after twenty years, I distinctly recall sitting in a circle with a group of children who attended a Safeplace support group. Daniel opened that discussion by saying, "Welcome to Kids Group. Some of us have been hurt by people in our families and people we know. Here in Kid's Group there is no violence. This is a safe place to talk about our experiences and to play." His moving words touched me as I gazed at the circle of boys and girls. I learned the power of simple honesty for my work with children; and it has carried over to my work with adult men.

Women who work in the field of sexual assault and domestic violence can find it difficult to work with male professionals. Even men with long experience in this work may unconsciously display sexist beliefs and behaviors. This inadvertent betrayal of trust can reinforce the feeling that men can't change. How will women respond to a newcomer when he makes his first sexist mistake? Will they see it as a teachable moment? No matter how women respond, we have a continuing responsibility to reeducate ourselves. Unlearning a lifetime of sexism is our work and an ongoing process.

One in four female professionals has survived rape and/or abuse at the hands of men. The percentage may be even larger for women who work as community sexual assault/domestic violence advocates and educators. Developing or regaining trust with men can be an ongoing issue for both women and men (who will probably make mistakes along the way.) The resulting tension between women and men in the profession, which is rarely addressed in the literature or in practice, limits the opportunity for male involvement in the field as it is now structured. I raise the issue because of the likelihood that practitioners who are reading this book will experience the phenomenon. Were it not for the patient support of the women at Safeplace, I would not be doing this work today. Although difficult to do, they showed understanding and compassion for me as I earnestly made an effort to become allied with women in the movement. They suffered my gender-biased blunders and guided my entry into a realm of heightened awareness. I would like to think that I helped validate their trust in men.

In *Race Matters,* Cornell West wrote, "Quality leadership is neither the product of one great individual nor the result of odd historical accidents. Rather it comes from deeply bred traditions and communities that shape and mold talented and gifted people" (2001, p.37). Everyone profits from men's enlightened involvement in VP. Compassionate mentoring by women can forever change the lives of men. I am a man who grew up playing hockey in the Midwest: if I can change, any man can.

It is men who must teach men if violence is to be reduced on a large scale. Men bring a valued presence that often accelerates the change process simply because they are men. Male educators bring insights, lived experience and credibility to the conversation of male violence against women. Warranted or not, men often have a higher valued currency with impressionable young men than do female educators.

Male mentors' moral convictions can galvanize boys' attentions and provide them with an alternative view of masculinity, while sparking insightful reflection on male stereotypes. Men can work easily in fraternity houses, male athletic settings and other male social groups. When men work together mindfully and openly discuss how restrictive male roles can suppress their best characteristics, they can increase their solidarity with women. When men share stories of their girlfriends, sisters and mothers who have survived male violence, it helps them understand how rape and battery hurt men as well as women.

Questions that the reader should consider include:

- What are my beliefs about working with men?

- Do I tend to see men as allies or adversaries in my work?

- When I work with men, do I look for their potential or anticipate their inadequacies?

I recommend spending ninety percent of your energy on positive solutions and no more than ten percent on negative difficulties. If you view men as an unredeemable hindrance, let go of that limiting belief and begin to embrace a view of men with unlimited possibilities. High-school and college students, police officers, coaches, teachers and fraternity presidents – even reformed gang members – are an incredibly rich and untapped resource for stopping rape and abuse. If you wish to inspire men to become leaders in prevention you must assume that they will both understand and accept their roles.

I seek to move men to address and change predominantly male norms that equate strength in men with dominance over women. Domination of women can never be a part of being a strong man. We must create cultural discourse about who initiates domestic violence and sexual assault. Although many participants in my workshops acknowledge knowing a survivor of rape or abuse, they rarely discuss knowing the perpetrators of these crimes – another indication of how we dodge the fundamental issue of male responsibility. Robert, a sophomore in a small Alabama college, affirmed this view: "I think men need a forum to talk about the fact that we are the ones who perpetuate most of the violence and how this affects our psyche."

Educators and the media are much more comfortable discussing how women can protect themselves against perpetrators than they are discussing the fact that a rapist may be the classmate, co-worker or the guy next door. Our societal approach to preventing violence fails in part because of its over-riding focus on women victims and an accompanying emphasis on the legal repercussions for perpetrators – approaches that are tertiary at best.

The idea of accepting responsibility pushes a button of defensiveness in some men. It certainly did in me twenty years ago. Even professionals are not immune to defensiveness about male responsibility. I remember proposing an MVP pilot program to a Washington State Department of Education male administrator and a group of female colleagues. When I introduced the subject of men acknowledging responsibility for their actions and the need to reexamine current ideas of masculinity, the administrator countered with, "What about all the women in prison for violence?" I could have pointed to the twenty-to-one male-to-female imbalance in the prison population (Greenfield, 1997, p.15-17). I could have cited the disproportionately large ratio of violent crimes committed by men. But I chose not to try to make either point because I sensed an unwillingness on his part to collaborate. Unfortunately his power, gender, and political stature meant that the women in the group – several of whom later privately supported my position – could not openly oppose his misinformed position.

Increasing men's understanding enables them to be honest with themselves about the central issues that underpin violence. It is men who rape and abuse women, and it is men who can be inspired to work with their peers to stop it. So, how can we enlist men in this work? The next chapter reveals how the culture of contemporary music can serve as an innovative avenue for teaching young men to become allies and mentors in violence prevention.

THREE

Telling Is Not Teaching: Using Music to Engage and Educate Students

Tell me and I will forget.
Show me and I will remember.
Involve me and I will understand.

RESEARCHERS AGREE THAT SEXUAL AND DOMESTIC VIOLENCE is a continuing problem in our homes and communities, and on our campuses. One in three women worldwide will be raped, beaten, or abused during the course of their lives (Collins et al, 1999). Although there is increasingly widespread discussion of the need to involve men in prevention programs, innovation has been missing in our approaches to educate men about the complex issues that underpin male violence.

Our first encounter with students in prevention programs is usually our last opportunity to move them to become involved in a sustained manner. I have learned that music can be a powerful tool to reeducate young men (and women) regarding violence.

Telling is not necessarily teaching. Lectures are almost always lethal in prevention education. An inventive way to inspire student participation is to teach them how to set their poetry to the music of youth-culture. A reasonable concern is that the media promote music with lyrics that encourage violence. Much has been written about the strong influence that television, movies, video games, and music have on us all. The media are a huge, largely unregulated multibillion-dollar industry – and violence sells! I am unconvinced by the claim that the principal influence on teaching violence to youth is the media. My experience is that the media have less influence on children than their early family experiences do. When the family solves problems nonviolently and reinforces peaceful behaviors in the child, the influence of the media is lessened.

We are nevertheless faced with the reality that media enter homes where abuse is already prevalent and provide fuel to the fire of learned violent behavior. Homes characterized by divorce after divorce, unstable relationships among adults, domestic violence, sexual assault, and alcohol/drug abuse take a far greater toll on youth than do the media or the lyrics of hip-hop music. It is a gross oversimplification to blame the media for the continuation of male violence in the United States. Research on the influence of media violence is inconclusive and contradictory. Blaming the media is yet another way by which we avoid addressing the uncomfortable underpinning issue of male responsibility for domestic violence and sexual abuse. Interpersonal violence in our culture occurred long before the advent of radio, television or film.

Let's look at the situation positively: although our youth are exposed to enormous amounts of media violence, a vast majority of them do *not* engage in violence. Additionally, millions of youth are rejecting corporate media and consumerism and are exploring alternative cultures. They are skeptical and often critical of maintream media as their source of information. Nevertheless, we should pay careful attention to the children who have been fed a steady diet of media violence. It is important to note that I refer both to children of color who live in poverty and to a large fraction of our white youth in affluent homes where supervision is minimal and violence is reinforced as acceptable behavior. Violence knows no social class or racial barriers – nor does contemporary music. One creative solution for engaging youth in prevention education lies with using the media!

Seeing the potential of music as the principal carrier of my message of nonviolent conflict resolution, I developed a successful approach for engaging men, boys, and girls in our work. In 1995 I was seeking new ways to increase the involvement of students I had been educating for the past decade. I sought to engage them through their own culture. Seeing youth with their portable Walkmans, I recognized that kids' music was no longer limited to their homes and cars – it had become a part of their lives anywhere and anytime. (With the advent of iPods, cell phones, and satellite radio the variety and availability of music will continue to accelerate.)

I created a pilot mix of songs that addressed racism, sexism, male violence, and sexual assault and previewed them during in-service training with a large group of middle/high school teachers in the Tacoma, Washington school district. The educators enthusiastically responded to it.

A subsequent classroom presentation in a diverse Spokane middle school confirmed my growing belief in the potential of music to engage students in VP education. During a week-long residency I started a workshop with a group of "behavior-disorder" boys. As I scanned my class of dreary-eyed students, I realized I had to adapt my presentation to the instructional setting. I took a risk and improvised a free-style rap introduction, instead of following my lesson plan. It went something like this:

"This classroom session is about violence prevention,
So listen up, I want your attention
You can rap with me, or serve another detention
Now my vocal skills are a bit lacking
I'm looking for help and some MC backing
Speak to me about the challenges you face,
I'm talkin' about gender, class, culture and race."

My impromptu musical introduction took the boys by surprise and ignited a forty-minute, freewheeling, session on a variety of topics including school and community violence, bullying, race, and school suspensions. Students quickly picked up on the idea and began creating their individual raps and subsequently listening closely to one another's insightful musical offerings.

One astonished teacher pulled me aside at the program's conclusion and remarked, "I have never seen the boys so engaged by any program!" I knew I was onto something with this unique musical approach to education. During the course of my residency, other students (and teachers) asked if I was going to present my "rapping program" to their class. News of the "behavior disorder" music session had spread throughout the school. Students were promoting the idea with other students.

I found the environment and resources to take my music program to the next level in my own backyard. I already was aware of the impact Olympia, Washington was having on the contemporary music industry. Groups like Nirvana and Sleater-Kinney (Time magazine's selection as the best rock band of 2001) emerged from Olympia. The local thriving music community further piqued my interest to find musical ways to involve youth.

Working with young men in their own language, and specifically using music, were the keys to involving a diverse variety of community, school, and college men in our MVP music project. We created innovative music, made a CD and toured western America presenting our programs to thousands of enthusiastic students. I was in search of a streetwise rapper to collaborate with our core group of musicians. Student evaluations and focus groups also suggested the need for a rapper to move our project to the next level. I attended an urban arts hip-hop music festival and heard Terrance, a talented young rapper. Terrance's political approach in his rap music intrigued me, since it did not include misogynistic lyrics. When I approached him with my idea of MVP music, he was skeptical but he agreed to listen to our pilot music CD. That was the beginning of a year-long internship for an exceptional musician who had grown up in juvenile prison. It is doubtful that I could have interested any reformed gang member with a standard, lecture approach to VP – but the idea of using rap music to educate his peers appealed to him.

The Evergreen State College magazine featured the evolution of our MVP music (Shé, 2002).

It's about You, Man

> "Music by men, for men." So go the first words on the CD, *Between the Beats.* What's New? Most music is by men for men, as are films, television, advertising – media, period. But this is different. This CD is the brainchild of Todd Denny, The Evergreen State College (TESC) grad '85, and part of the Men's Violence Prevention Music Project (MVP). In the song 'Fear Economy,' MVP exhorts you to 'Raise your glasses to the fear economy: war, professional sports and pornography. Timber, television and the prison industry.

Corporate music, alcohol and gasoline.' Eerily apt, in light of the events on September 11. Now, more than ever, boys and men need nonviolent role models. And Denny wants to provide them.

Denny also wants to make rape and domestic violence a male issue. 'For 30 years it's been a women's issue. That defies common logic. We've got to stop de-gendering violence. It's not teen violence or gang violence – it's male violence.' Full of stats and facts, he reels off that mostly boys and men, ages 13 to 29, are responsible for the majority of violent acts in our society. Why, then, is this labeled a women's issue? He doesn't wait around for an answer. Instead, he's crafted a program to reach those 13 to 29 year-olds with music. Music not only soothes the savage beast, it makes him change his behavior, or so Denny believes. MVP's musical messages are simple, with good rappin' beats: treat women well, look out for other humans, that woman in Playboy is somebody's mother, sister, or daughter, and intervene if you see something dangerous about to happen.

Like many a Greener after him, Denny interned at Safeplace, the rape relief and women's shelter in Olympia. 'I wouldn't be where I am today without Safeplace,' Denny says. The position initially called for basic childcare, but while he was there, Denny developed activities to help children cope with abuse. When the mothers went off to discuss domestic violence issues with Safeplace counselors, Denny spent the time with the children – an hour of coping and expressing activities, another hour playing "just for fun."

Denny's mentor says the Greener is ahead of his time. "He's on the cutting edge, using popular culture to educate people about male violence. The hardest thing is to make people aware of their socialization, especially teenagers. MVP is very effective," says Fred Schrumpf, student services coordinator for the Spokane Public School District.

Passionate about primary prevention, Denny goes to the source of the violence problem – men. 'Our ideas of masculinity have to change. People are desperate. The catalyst for me was all the school shootings. They were mostly done by suburban white boys who had been bullied and harassed. We [MVP] offer primary prevention, not secondary, not tertiary. We are all about creating new opportunities and looking for new expectations.'

Like rap. One day during one of his anti-violence programs, Denny started rapping spontaneously. The kids joined in, and afterwards, he heard them making up their own anti-violence raps. 'That's when I knew I was on to something.'

That initial rap session led to a CD, but Denny thought he sounded too white, too straight, and too old. His fears were affirmed by the evaluations he received, which suggested he 'Get rid of the white guy.' He realized if he wanted to do this right, he had to have the right musicians. He heard about a rapper-poet-artist named Terrance, and a rapping cowboy from Montana named Sandman. Enter Terrance and Chris "Sandman" Sand. They listened to Denny's spiel, liked his ideas, and hopped aboard the MVP Music Project. Add

> Adrian Martinez to the literal mix (current Greener, musician and recording engineer), and boom, you've got driving beats without hit-me-over-the-head messages. 'We're getting close to something great,' Denny says. And when I find myself singing the lyrics to 'Fear Economy' I have to agree.

The project that Elizabeth Shé describes evolved into our middle and high school "Gear Up with Music" (GUM) Program, funded by the U.S. Department of Education. Our school program engages boys and girls in violence prevention leadership and encourages them to plan for college. Post secondary education is an important tool in breaking the cycle of violence. We create opportunities for students to develop and use their own voice to assert their inner feelings about violence. Our week-long school music residency (GUM) brings boys and girls together to work in music teams to create songs that address challenging personal subjects such as bullying, sexual abuse, racism, gangs, school violence, alcohol and drugs.

Students see that these issues inhibit their safety, personal growth, and success both in and out of school. Working together in cooperative groups meets kids' needs and enhances their sense of belonging and power. They work harder in groups, learn more by supporting each another, and have fun in the process. Students enthusiastically participate in our literacy and writing project, which empowers them through the medium of popular culture. Boys and girls love to have their voices heard, and they heartily accept the role of mentoring their peers. Their efforts are further reinforced, and their commitment enhanced, by the recognition they receive from classmates, teachers, and administrators. When a music team performs the song they created on the subject of the pitfalls of gang life, their peers listen with rapt attention.

My residency program demonstrates how youth culture's own language can be used to convey lasting, positive images. Nurturing youth within our cultural "soup" of family, peers, school and media is a complex task; but it is incredibly rewarding to witness student voices replace machismo, aggression and sexism with uplifting, positive messages.

GUM has broad applicability; it has been successfully implemented with Mexican-American youth in one of San Diego's poorest middle schools; on the Yakima Indian reservation in rural Washington; African-American students in Tacoma; and with Caucasian students mixed with students of color in all our residencies.

The project is educationally unique because it is rooted in students' work rather than in media adults create for young learners. Music opens students' imagination to new freedoms of form and content. Lyrics emerge from their own inner world and culture. These learners give form to dreams and experiences at important stages of their lives. After a decade of facilitating this program, I still find myself inspired by the varied and unique content of students' songs. Another plus is that other students enthusiastically receive youth-created music. The residency culminates with music teams' recording their songs and poetry devoted to preventing violence onto a CD. When students then present their songs live to their peers it's a "can't-miss" experience! "Gear Up with Music" CDs have had multiple uses in the students' schools, local radio stations and communities.

Writing, literacy, and language arts are key curricular vehicles we employ in our music programs. We do not rely on lectures or visual presentations drawn from an adult cultural perspective. Working in teams, students create and record a series of songs and rhythmic presentations that successfully address volatile and tough issues about violence. Through immersion in writing, students create authentic stories about their own lives; the stories that evolve into songs that are their own! This program has become a lighthouse project – an exemplary beacon with students leading the way to reduce the violence that limits their opportunity to succeed in life.

Our music program focuses on four key areas: (1) social-behavioral curricula in schools, (2) peer leadership (designed to increase resistance to peer pressure and to develop competent social skills, (3) community-wide activities designed to change the larger environment (mass media campaign), and (4) parental involvement/education.

"Gear Up with Music" also integrates and reinforces the English-language arts and state content standards for K-12 schools in many states. When students vigorously draft, read and rewrite their lyrics and create songs with a team of their peers we have a powerful instructional tool for both learners and teachers. Students acquire skills needed for classroom presentations to speak out against and prevent peer abuse. We have learned from middle/high school youth throughout the United States how music can be a valuable carrier of a positive view of culture.

Our residency unfolds as follows:

Before our arrival, the school announces and posts "Gear Up with Music" flyers to inform students about our program. Student interest and response is typically immediate and enthusiastic. We limit the residency class size to approximately forty students to enhance the quality of our mentoring. We randomly assign students to songwriting groups so they can develop new relationships, work closely with their peers, and to keep them on task. By arbitrarily grouping writers we foster team camaraderie and reinforce the concept of students as allies with both friends and strangers. During the first two days, we introduce students to the idea of using music to improve their writing skills, as well as to the broad idea of violence prevention education.

Our residency team includes a recording engineer and a guest musician, both of whom work closely with the young songwriters. As the third member of the team, I conduct three separate student workshops that address:

- violence in the home,
- the role of "masculinity" in conflict and violence, and
- the media as a tool in violence prevention education.

Each workshop includes a teacher's lesson plan to prompt further discussion and introspection within the students' regular classrooms (see Appendix A). Students keep a journal of their workshop and life experiences, and their journal notes evolve into songs and poetry. On the third day we introduce musical "Beats," a collection of instrumental tunes as a guide for students to craft their lyrics and songs. Students also produce "Peace at Our School" commercials for use in public service announcements.

During our residency we assist the student groups while they identify themes, craft lyrics and fine-tune their songs. Working in small teams of three to six songwriters, most groups decide to include all members' voices in the recording process. Others have individuals who write lyrics only or create art and design for the CD cover. We consider the students' interests and abilities and ensure individual involvement in a variety of areas. Our sound engineer mentors a select group of students who express interest in developing recording skills and pursuing a career in his field. We consciously involve equal proportions of girls and boys in what is too often a male-dominated aspect of the profession.

We nurture and support our core group of serious, young songwriters throughout the week as they continue to craft and practice their songs during lunch time and even in their homes during the evenings. Such behavior is gratifying because it departs from the expectations about homework that we often have for middle/ high school youth. With parental approval GUM carries over into the students' homes. Imagine students voluntarily working in teams after school and proudly bringing their "homework" to show their parents: a finished violence prevention music CD.

During the final two days, students put the finishing touches on their songs as they excitedly prepare for their performance, at an assigned recording time. Students may record in a language other than English as well, e.g., Spanish. Before mastering the CDs, our sound engineer works closely with the music teams and provides helpful recording technique suggestions. Students excitedly and proudly receive a copy of their musical CD, which includes their picture and songwriting credits.

The residency culminates with a final day of celebration with student teams presenting a live music show to their peers. With our coaching they continue to perform their music in other classrooms, school assemblies and the community. High school students present to neighboring middle schools. Middle school teams present to area elementary schools. Our program is sustainable, transferable, and designed to continue long after our departure. "Gear Up with Music" successfully engages students from diverse racial and demographic backgrounds because it capitalizes on the value that youth place on music as a carrier of their culture.

Another benefit of our musical approach to peer education is the enhancement of school climate and safety by empowering students to be on the frontline of prevention. This occurs when music teams present to classrooms, assemblies, and community groups. Schools' current reliance on video cameras, dress codes, metal detectors, and police don't make students feel safer in school. Youth do feel safer and empowered when adults listen to their voices and their concerns. Many campuses have used student-created songs on their school announcement system as a peer education tool. Imagine the start of a school day when students (and teachers) listen to a song about creating peace in their school – a song written and performed by a member of the student body! Consider the following lyrics in one such song entitled, "The Cards We Were Dealt." Middle school, high school and college students have resonated positively to its message.

The cards we were dealt
For instance ethnicity
Gender, class, culture and ability
Stereotypes, prejudice, discrimination
Some lack money, some education.

Some get the ace, the king and the queen
While others get jack, if you know what I mean
Some get the two, the three, maybe a four
Some get the full house and pretend to be poor.

Some go to war, some go to prison
Some go to Ivy League schools and
Some go fishin'.

Some get the royal flush, some get flushed, but
The ones with the money like to keep it all hush, hush

Some people sink, some float to the top
But the dealer keeps dealing and the game don't stop
Nobody wins, whether you think so or not
And the dealer keeps dealing and the game don't stop.

(Girl's solo by Nancy Rivera, Toppenish High, Toppenish, WA follows.)

I come from the streets of LBC (Long Beach, CA) and
I know I ain't Snoop D O double G,
But somehow, someway
I came to Toppenish at the age of 2
My mom and my dad didn't know what to do
Broke up, separated, left me with the blues
Now 15 years, all dazed and confused.

Gear Up support is what I have used
To pick my path. Be smart with the one you choose
Don't pick the wrong way, you don't want to lose
My mom didn't raise no fools,
Even as a single mother she used the right tools
Working hard, living poor and going to school
We worked our way up and now it's all cool.

Now I'm gonna let you go
Before I drop, drop, drop like a top
So bye, bye, bye
This is where I stop.

(Boy's solo by Martin Cuevas, Toppenish High, Toppenish, WA follows.)

Hey y'all, check it out
I was born in LA, where we don't play
Gotta keep your eyes open like every day
People always getting shot on every corner of the street
Gonna spit the rhyme of my life to Giles beat
Now I'm in the T O P P E N I S H
Gonna kick my verse and front, not a fake
Thinking life was fine, living life without my father
No advice to turn to made life harder.

I turned to my beloved mother asked her why
What she responded with always made me cry
So you see I grew up not knowing my dad
Missing all the good time we could have had
Decided to get wise and go to school
Didn't want to end up on the street as a fool.

See, don't take education for granted, it's a
valuable tool
I was raised on what we could only afford
Watching other people play like a Honda Accord
But thanks to my mother, she knew the way
With her love and support, I made it to this day
So you see you can learn a lot of lessons in life
I was dealt the cards of everything
What I have to figure out is
What to put down and what to play.

Our innovative prevention work evolved into a musical video collaboration with the Washington State Attorney General's Office, a staff member of which attended an MVP music presentation and was won over by our unique approach. The Attorney General's Office was seeking a new way to involve youth on the issue of interpersonal violence. Previously they had printed 5,000 pamphlets for teens. We recruited high school students as peer educators. Two young men and one woman starred in the music video entitled, "Hands Are Not for Hurting."

The video portrays a young man who was controlling, jealous, and physically abusive to his girlfriend. Our project involved students in each phase including; preproduction, assisting in script development and lyrics writing and acting in the video. We developed classroom lesson plans for teachers to examine the video and help students to develop intervention skills for use in abusive situations. We also developed evaluation instruments for both students and teachers to help us assess the video's effectiveness. Students and educators decided the video was a better fit for middle school students than for older kids because of the actors' ages. The "Hands" music video is currently available on the internet (Denny, 2003).

"Hands" lyrics, created in our workshops, are:

(Chorus) Hands are not for hurting, they're for loving and touching
Holding hands in the sand and for playing percussion
Hands are for clapping, not for giving concussions
These words should be heard, so let's have a discussion.

(Verse) Here's a little story about Jimmy and Susan,
Boyfriend/girlfriend, Friday night cruisin'
Around downtown and it's getting late
When Susan runs into someone she used to date.
Nothing serious, just old flames,
But Jimmy gets jealous and starts calling Susan names.
He's just joking you say, What a silly thought
You and your buddies think it's funny, but it's really not.

(Chorus) Hands are not for hurting, they're for loving and touching…

(Verse) Relationships begin with a connection that's strong
But sometimes they unravel and things can go wrong.
Jealousy, control become the norm
Like walking on eggshells, always weathering a storm.

(Verse) Here's another story I just got out of court.
I was on the jury, so allow me to report
What I heard, what I saw.
Jimmy punched Susan, he broke the law
And Susan called the cops, her face was raw.
Plus she had witnesses, Jimmy broke his hand, but still
He's pleading innocent.
He's got stitches on his knuckles to prove that violence hurts everyone,
He must have not have known that.

(Chorus) Hands are not for hurting, they're for loving and touching…

(Verse) Yo, hands are for good things, they're positive
You can like shake hands, play guitar
Throw a Frisbee, grip the microphone
Click a mouse, slap a cross fader
Take a photograph, whatever
Play ball, shift gears, and grab the steering wheel.
Change CD's, mini discs, cell phones,
Whatever; they're hands, they're all good.

If you feel controlled, pressured or afraid
Then that's not love, more like a hand grenade
Waiting to explode and you get hurt
Physically and emotionally you feel like dirt
Love is about sweetness, cherishing the soul
It's pure and easy, not about control
Control, control, control.

(Chorus) Hands are not for hurting, they're for loving and touching…

The MVP music project also addresses how homophobia contributes to the culture of male violence. We examine how young men often carefully monitor their peers' "unmasculine" qualities so they can ridicule them. "That's gay" is a prevalent critique for unacceptable behavior and used as a tool to keep boys 'in line' to conform to culturally-endorsed, male stereotypes.

The "Homophobia" lyrics are;

> If you think about it, calling someone gay or a fag is one of the biggest putdowns for guys today. Homophobic and antigay prejudices and behaviors contribute to a lot of violence in both boys and men by our constant proving of our heterosexuality. Homophobia prevents many guys from expressing their true selves, for fear their actions will be labeled as "gay." For example, I grew up playing ice hockey. But let's suppose instead of hockey I decided to take up something like figure skating. Do you think my peers would have treated me differently? I think so and I'd bet some of that treatment would have been abusive. (Note: in Europe figure skating for men is considered to be a strong and masculine sport).
>
> Gay youth commit two-thirds of all teen suicides. Is there a genetic predisposition for gay people to want to take their own lives? I don't think so. I think homophobia has much more to do with the fears, shame, and embarrassment our culture tries to associate with being gay. Homophobia hurts all of us, both gay and straight. Challenge homophobia!

Two spoken-word pieces, titled "Courage I" and "Courage II" are in the MVP music project. Here is one of them:

> Jackie Robinson became the first African-American major league baseball player (1947) – and it didn't happen easily. As a matter of fact there were sixteen major league teams back then and their owners voted fifteen-to-one against

letting blacks play in the majors. The lone dissenting team was the Brooklyn Dodgers, the team that Jackie would play for. Branch Rickey, the owner of the Dodgers, somehow convinced the other owners that the world wouldn't come to an end if Robinson played.

That first year was anything but a cake walk for Robinson since he was consistently ridiculed, belittled, and verbally harassed at baseball stadiums all around our great nation. He received no encouragement from any players on the other teams. About halfway through that first season something happened that turned the history of major league baseball around. Imagine this: during the middle of a particularly hostile game, as Jackie was being mercilessly taunted by the crowd of about 30,000 fans, the shortstop on his team, a white guy from Kentucky by the name of Pee Wee Reese walked across the infield during the middle of the game and put his arm around Jackie. The crowd was stunned, the hostile voices grew silent, everyone was wondering what was going on? That moment revealed the power of courage to transform attitudes. They were in it together, black and white; friends, teammates, and the Brooklyn Dodgers. That proved to be a turning point in the growing acceptance of Jackie Robinson, not only by the fans, but also by opposing teams and some of his teammates.

There are at least three examples of courage in that story. First you have an owner who went against the tide of rival owners. Second, you have Pee Wee Reese, a white guy from Kentucky taking a stand for what was right regardless of its

> unpopularity. And third, we have Jackie Robinson who took the risks and abuse that came with his breaking the color barrier in major league baseball.
>
> Real courage is having the guts to confront and speak out against what is wrong, be it in baseball or men's abuse of women. Whether it is sexual harassment or sexual assault, I think it's up to us guys to take the lead. So tell me: how do you define courage?

Violence prevention education can involve students in a compelling, nondidactic way, as contrasted with the typically dull rehearsals of problems by adults. Tell students about VP and they just might fall asleep. Involve them with an approach such as creating music that includes activities that address the problem in their idiom, and they might become lifelong allies.

By now you may be wondering how to start a VP program on your campus, in your school, or in your community. In the following chapter I detail the tactics and describe the exercises I use to teach rape prevention skills in my workshops.

FOUR

How to Begin a Workshop

*I never ask a program participant to do anything
I wouldn't feel comfortable doing myself.*

THIS CHAPTER OFFERS PEDAGOGICAL SUGGESTIONS for use in your violence prevention workshops with men. There are additional ways to engage men, of course; but whatever method you choose, be candid, supportive, and participate in the discussions and exercises.

Within the first three minutes of every program I facilitate, I engage men in a highly interactive discussion of an issue relating to gender roles, masculinity, sexual harassment, or alcohol and drugs (interconnected topics which contribute to sexual assault). I use a chronological lifeline of the men's learned behaviors to address any issue when examining men's violence against women. Utilizing a series of small group exercises and scenarios, I encourage men to develop VP strategies to gain a sense of empathy for sexual assault survivors and to elicit peer support for confronting male violence.

When a fraternity president, football player, or former gang member speaks, he generally commands the respect and attention of his peers. For many participants it is their first experience of connecting with other men who share similar values and beliefs. As Paul, an athlete at the University of Wisconsin, succinctly stated during an MVP workshop, "There are guys who really do care about how something like rape can affect women." My work creates a forum that empowers men to learn nonviolent skills that rely on their intellect and not their brawn.

Many men have witnessed abuse against women but have felt powerless or unable to help. Our inability to take action reinforces our inadequacies in abusive situations – even if we want to do the right thing. At the heart of my work is this simple fact: we lose men as allies because of the limited opportunities they have to develop rape-prevention skills. By implementing an experiential, rather than lecture-based approach, I capture men's attention and elicit their involvement in creating interventions. And so can you!

Violence prevention educators should use their personal experiences as a catalyst for engaging men in discussions. Because intimacy involves risks, I follow this rule: I never ask a program participant to do anything I wouldn't feel comfortable doing myself. I've found that I am able to create trust and open dialogue by sharing my personal stories. Men respond to such honesty by opening up themselves.

Peer-based interventions empower men who have not experienced the role of being an ally in rape prevention. Hypermasculine men can reinforce myths such as, "She says No, when really she means Yes." After participating in an MVP exercise at a Wyoming community college, Vince candidly declared, "When a woman says 'No', it doesn't matter *how* it was said. All us guys must understand that or there is a violation happening."

The program must include the transformation of educators from viewing males solely as perpetrators of violence to seeing them as partners in prevention. This shift in viewpoint increases the trainer's capacity for involvement and his ability to benefit personally from the programs. Men respond enthusiastically when they assume leadership roles. Curtis, a freshman at a Missouri University, made an affirming comment in a large mixed-gender workshop: "As men we cannot rescue women. What we can do is stand up for our own beliefs about rape when dealing with other men."

I have four principal goals for my male violence prevention workshops. I want participants to:

- experience empathy for survivors of sexual assault,
- examine the essence of personal responsibility,
- develop practical skills for confronting sexually-aggressive peers, and
- understand how rape hurts men as well as women.

Were I to plunge into advanced training at the outset of a workshop, most men would find it difficult to accept because they are not ready to confront the tough issues. My approach is to help men recognize gradually their own deeper philosophical and personal concerns. It is an ongoing process that gives participants an opportunity to make connections between early life experiences and sexual aggression.

The following introductory exercise is adapted from the Oakland Men's Project (see my Introduction). It serves as a workshop icebreaker and helps men understand how their life experiences have shaped their views of sexual aggression. I begin by reading a series of statements, asking them to please stand if a statement applies to them. I emphasize that everyone has a right to participate in this exercise only to the extent that he chooses. [Note: I sit in a chair and participate by rising whenever a statement applies to me.]

I begin by reading, "Please stand up if you would rather not be here."

(Several men will stand, evoking laughter and relieving tension. I commend them for their honesty and ask for this type of candor, along with respect, throughout our workshop.)

It is worth noting that unplanned, humorous moments often serve as program "icebreakers." While I was introducing a date-rape workshop with a fraternity at the University of Illinois, a member stood up, looked around at his brothers and observed, "I don't know if you noticed, but we're not the best-looking house on campus. Some of us can't even get a date." Another member immediately exclaimed, "Speak for yourself!" We all laughed, which helped cut group tension before moving on to the important work that lay ahead.

I continue: "Please stand up if you are on a scholarship, either academic or athletic."

(I ask those who stand to tell us the field of study or sport with which they are involved.)

Moving on to the program's theme, I ask, "Have you ever heard antifemale comments in your home, at school, or from friends at some point in your life?"

(Most of the men stand. I point out that these demeaning comments are often our earliest experience in misogynistic acculturation.)

This is followed by, "Have you ever felt pressure from friends to affirm your sexual prowess or to brag about your success?

You might have been asked questions like:

* How did the date go?
* Are you going out again?
* Did you kiss her?
* Did you get any?

(I usually share a personal experience about dating and feeling peer pressure, which warms up the group for contributing their personal anecdotes to the general discussion. You, too, might wish to share a personal story to spark conversation.)

Mark, a high school junior, comments,

> "Last year my friends would constantly inquire and try to probe into details of my dating experiences. It made me feel uncomfortable; it was a personal issue that I didn't feel the need to discuss."

Jonathon, a college senior, adds,

> "As a male in our culture I feel broadsided by peers and by the portrayal of women in the media. Those messages are both powerful and corrupt. They put pressure on us guys to be sexually active and successful."

As others rise to offer their comments, I prompt further discussion by asking, "Have you ever been stereotyped, judged, or unfairly targeted as a male in our culture?"

Michael, a fraternity member, speaks:

"I feel we men get stereotyped often, even though we aren't all bad."

Luis, a student athlete, remarks,

"Why should I feel guilty for being a man, when I personally have not committed a crime?"

I often hear similar remarks in my MVP workshops and validate them with a neutral comment such as, "Good question. I promise that we will discuss that during the workshop." (The program moves beyond guilt to develop male leadership.)

Then I ask, "Do you know a survivor of rape or child abuse?"

(More then half the men can be expected to stand.)

Robert, a junior, shared his story.

"My girlfriend was raped on campus. It made me feel really mad and helpless. I wanted him to be punished or maybe even hurt really badly."

Lucas, a high-school sophomore, revealed his feelings about a rape survivor in this story fragment:

"A really good girlfriend of mine was raped. I felt angry and shocked. I wish she had told me first, instead of someone else."

During my workshop I encourage men to record their stories. A participant wrote this confidential experience:

> "My sister's apartment was broken into and she was raped. I felt anger, pain, and helplessness. I wanted justice."

A fraternity member anonymously shared another chilling story during a MVP workshop:

> "I was raped by two older neighbor boys when I was in the 5th grade. I was ashamed, confused and felt paralyzed for years afterward. I wanted support to be able to come forward to reveal the assault. I didn't know who I could talk to."

His shocking story reinforces the fact that millions of men are also survivors of sexual violence. Approximately one in ten men is a victim, often in the form of child sexual abuse. A survey found that males constituted "15% of juvenile sexual assault victims with an object, 20% of the juvenile victims of forcible fondling, and 59% of the juvenile victims of forcible sodomy." Furthermore, "The year in a male's life when he is most likely to be a victim of sexual assault is age 4" (Snyder, 2000, p.4).

By the time they are seniors in high school, the majority of men have friends, sisters, or girlfriends who have survived sexual assault. Awareness of these life experiences heightens their empathy, positioning them to be leaders in stopping violence against women.

I point out that we probably all know a survivor because we all know four women. Furthermore, we are even more unaware of how widespread the problem is because many rape victims remain silent. Less than five percent of completed and attempted rapes of college students are reported to law enforcement (Karjane, Fisher, 2005, p.10). I discuss how the high prevalence of acquaintance rape creates apprehension in both victimized and nonvictimized women when they are developing relationships with men. Since most rape perpetrators are acquaintances, e.g., male friends, classmates or co-workers, women understandably wonder, "Can I trust any man?" Part of the coercion that functions in acquaintance rape is a presumed shared level of trust on the part of the woman. Trust is one of many unspoken assumptions that underpin new relationships for women and men. Andy, a Seattle community college MVP workshop participant, voiced a similar sentiment, "As a man I am learning how to trust, too. I want to learn how to trust more."

The desire to develop an intimate relationship is something many men strive toward. Men need to understand that a woman's rape experience drastically impairs her ability to develop trusting relationships. Acquaintance rape survivors can come to view *all* men as potential perpetrators. This stereotype is understandable given the pandemic levels of male violence committed against women in our communities and on our nation's campuses. Such mistrust also reinforces the point of how rape hurts men and women.

Are we an ally with women when we do nothing even when we are aware of friends who are rapists? I remind men that the victim could be their girlfriend, their sister, or even their mother. Personalization shows how rape affects all men and reinforces the premise that stopping rape is men's business.

Next I ask, "Has anyone ever done something to challenge or stop sexual aggression?"

(For some men, it will be the first time they have entertained the idea – much less heard other men discuss the need for male action.)

During a workshop I conducted for a Big Ten fraternity, Jeff, a senior, told this story to sixty members of his house:

> "I was once the president of another fraternity. I resigned and left my chapter after one of my 'brothers' sexually assaulted my girlfriend's best friend. I just couldn't continue in my leadership role knowing what had occurred and that despite my efforts to hold him accountable for the rape, he had not been punished."

Sixty men quietly reflected on Jeff's candid disclosure. Men like Jeff, who display leadership by challenging sexual assault, are vocal in my programs, to their benefit and that of their peers.

Alan Berkowitz told me the following story about a Brown University student who had the courage to confront abusive men.

> "I was walking across the quad late one night when I saw a group of men who were clearly harassing a woman. My impulse was to not get involved, especially because they seemed belligerent and I honestly was concerned for my safety. But I just had to do something, so I went up to the men pretending that I was lost. While I asked directions (to hold their attention) the woman was able to walk away."

My MVP workshops are predicated on the importance of working with men along a continuum of their life experiences. Do not plunge directly into the difficult and rarely discussed issue of sexual assault. Doing so understandably makes participants feel uncomfortable. Most men have neither examined nor discussed the subject with their peers. Working sequentially through men's life experiences in a safe and introspective manner helps prepare them to understand the underpinning factors that influence sexual assault.

Once men have discussed their personal experiences with sexual violence and heard others share similar stories within a supportive and interactive setting, they are prepared to examine issues more thoroughly. These deeper musings can initiate a process of profound personal change and increases the chances of their continued involvement in MVP. We must provide time to allow men's beliefs to grow.

Men commonly approach me at my program's conclusion, shake my hand and ask, "What else can we do?" When given the opportunity, men can create tactics and interventions that will lessen the chance that rape will occur in social situations. I turn to that topic next.

FIVE

Teaching Rape Prevention Skills to Men

We indirectly become complicit with sexual violence,
if we are aware of it and do not challenge it at some level.

AFTER WORKSHOP PARTICIPANTS HAVE OFFERED and examined their introductory personal reflections, two principal goals will guide my work:

* the first is to teach men the cognitive skills they need to confront abusive peers; and

* the second is to help them create an environment within which they can develop skills for such interventions.

Men are usually unprepared, hesitant and unable to act when they witness violence against women. I assist them to learn ways to be helpful in potentially violent settings. Men respond with enthusiasm to conceptualizing prevention as an issue of male leadership.

We explore creative interventions within scenarios that range from date to gang rape. After I randomly assign them to small groups I present an ambiguous date rape situation for their in-depth exploration.

It's important to work with teams of no more than four or five men. Small-group interactions afford ample discussion time and a safe space for men to talk candidly. There is less posturing, peer pressure, and flippancy when men can connect faces with comments and can more readily express their personal values. Random assignment of men to groups helps keep them on task and allows them to develop strong new alliances. Group work also reinforces the concept that all men can become allies in preventing rape, with both friends and strangers.

I pose a potential date rape situation to the men:

> You and another guy have been sharing a campus apartment for the past year. Your roommate has been talking about a certain woman in one of his classes, whom he is especially interested in meeting. And he finally has a date with her one evening. He gets dressed up for the big night out, is excited, and asks to borrow a nice shirt.
>
> You wish him a good time as he leaves for his date. You are staying in to study for a midterm exam. About midnight, as you prepare to sleep, you hear your roommate and his date return to your place. You're curious and stay up a bit, hearing bits and pieces of their conversation. You hear them mix a few drinks and overhear more conversation. A little more time passes and it sounds like you hear her saying "No, no!" After a while you think you hear her crying. The

> next morning at breakfast, feeling a bit perplexed about the previous night, you ask your roommate how the date went. He smiles and says, "It went great!"

I ask them several questions, including:

* What would their reactions be if they were in the situation?
* What would they be thinking and feeling?
* Would it be difficult to ask a roommate anything about the date?

It is important to allow men ample time to process their initial reactions and doubts. They wonder, "What can I say or do?" We have all experienced hesitancy when we felt unprepared to take any action.

It is the inclination of most men to rush into an intervention. I do not support their predisposition. Male acculturation encourages us to act without examining our feelings. I spend time discussing and exploring the participants' thoughts and their rationale for action or inaction.

Men who are new to thinking about rape prevention are commonly concerned with realistic questions. I never dismiss their concerns but welcome them as avenues for introspection and clarification. Illustrations of their concerns include:

* I'm not certain what really happened.
* Is this my business?
* He might get angry if I say anything.

- My intervention could ruin our relationship.
- Do I want to live with a rapist?
- Do I want to be a snitch on my roomy?

Men candidly discuss the difficulty of confronting a roommate who may have sexually assaulted his date. This type of deep reflection and insightful exchange is peer education at its best!

First, it is critical to have them discuss their feelings, to process why many men feel unable or unwilling to take action. These are not easy questions to answer. Most men have been or will be in such situations during their academic careers and lives. As a facilitator, I acknowledge and document each participant's thought by writing it on a dry erase board for all to see. The group collectively develops a greater degree of mutual understanding of the difficulties that underlie taking action in a potential sexual assault.

Second, I zero in on what, if anything, they could do to intervene in the situation or speak up in a nonviolent way. I allow ample time for the small groups to discuss the merits or pitfalls of potential action and circulate around the room supporting their earnest discussions about possible solutions. After ten to fifteen minutes of animated discussion time I solicit each group's ideas and document them on a large dry erase board for all to see. Men regularly devise creative interventions when they are placed in new roles as non-violent helpers, in lieu of their historical roles as perpetrators and combatants who use force to address violence. Encouragingly, many of the participants say they would not wait until the following morning to do something, (even though I have deliberately framed the scenario in terms of waiting.)

When a man stands and announces that his group decided they

would have taken action that evening, he models primary prevention and seizes the attention of the entire room. Examples of peer-developed tactics include:

* Getting up and going to the bathroom or making some noise in their shared apartment so the woman knows help could be available.

* Knocking on their roommate's door to borrow a book (for their test preparation) or asking for a music CD or cell phone.

* Asking if they would like to order some pizza.

* Knocking on the roommate's door and asking, "Is everything "OK?"

Other men suggest making probing comments to their roommate the next morning:

* Inquiring if he is going to see her again.

* Asking how the date really went.

* Saying directly that "It sounded a bit unusual last night (and asking) what happened?"

Other men suggest that they would try to find the woman to get her side of the story. Such tactics can be broken into primary, secondary, and tertiary levels of rape prevention. We discuss the triad of interventions with a focus on primary prevention. Acting with integrity, most men agree that intervening during the potential assault is the most important action. I next review their specific ideas and continue to reinforce the proposition that they, as men, are the experts on assessing the feasibility of their interventions.

I validate the challenges in and necessity for men's taking action in such situations. Each participant develops his own unique intervention tactics based on personal choice. The shared intention of workshop participants is to stop rape for the fundamental reason that they believe it is wrong. Excuses for unwillingness to intervene are discussed as choices that are often based on regard for personal safety or one's level of readiness. The progress that a man makes is determined in part by the workshop's format and his readiness for change.

The relationship between a MVP teacher and his group may produce tension because the teacher is trying to help learners change their beliefs and behaviors. This is to be expected. Having a mutually agreed upon set of principles and de-personalizing criticism reduces tension. Men come to understand that whenever a MVP teacher exposes a myth, they are not being attacked personally but are learning to become better men. Once men learn how to do this work, they often do it better then any teacher had hoped. However, they must remain open to continual improvement.

We discuss how we indirectly become complicit with sexual violence, if we are aware of it and we do not challenge it at some level. Silence and inaction perpetuate rape. Candid conversation among men can help them develop specific intervention skills for their future use. The only bad option is inaction.

Few men understand the legal definitions of sexual assault. Understanding these definitions reduces the possibility of their being perpetrators of rape; and women need to know them to reduce the likelihood of becoming a victim. My next chapter addresses that need.

SIX

Redefining Rape

Force is the difference between rape and romance.

Most college students (including those who have survived rape) do not know the law and fail to recognize behaviors that meet the legal definition of rape. Rape is penetration by force or threat of force. This includes penetration of any orifice or body opening (the vagina or anus) with the penis, fingers, or any other object. If someone were to use force to obtain oral sex, that act would constitute rape. Force is the difference between rape and romance: it's that simple. The law does not weigh whether one knows or does not know the victim. Further, the law requires consent, defined as a clear, freely-given, verbalized "Yes" to the act in question. Moreover, one cannot interpret nonverbal cues, body language, or the inaction of another as a form of consent.

The practice of using alcohol as a "tool" to break down sexual reluctance in a woman is a violation of the law. Students generally do not understand that an intoxicated person is unable to give legal consent. (I draw an analogy with drinking and driving, where the law considers one not to be of sound mind and body when under the influence of alcohol.) Most students are unaware that, under the law, coercion can include:

* talking someone into sex.
* using alcohol as a tool to break down sexual reluctance.
* making verbal threats without actually using physical violence.
* using body weight to hold a person down, and
* locking a door to prevent exit from a room.

These and other forms of coercion must be discussed and clarified. I remind students that alcohol use is not the "cause" of sexual violence. However it is a contributing factor, increases risk, the likelihood of greater physical injury to female victims, and is the primary rape drug. The real causes of sexual assault are the underpinning values, beliefs, and behaviors that I discuss during my workshop.

The federal code regarding rape is uniform but criminal statutes regarding rape vary from state to state. Redefinitions of sexual violence have occasionally readdressed ambiguities of language such as force and coercion. Sexual assault addresses broader, unwanted sexual activity including touching, fondling, kissing, and any other unwanted sexual contact with an individual's body; unwanted vaginal, anal, or oral penetration with any object; exposure and/or flashing of sexual body parts; forcing an individual to masturbate or to masturbate someone else; to perform or receive oral sex; to look at sexually explicit material and forcing an individual to pose for sexually explicit pictures.

Campus policy definitions of sexual assault should pay particular attention to

* sexual acts other than penile-vaginal penetration,
* the use of threats and coercive force as tools to victimize,
* taking advantage of a victim who is under the influence of alcohol and drugs,
* the need for gender neutrality; e.g., addressing the issue of men being victims of rape.

The literature related to male socialization is replete with stories of men misinterpreting a woman's behaviors as "flirtatious" when her intention is to be perceived as "friendly." This misperception occurs particularly in social occasions such as parties, bars, and dates. I create opportunities in my workshops for women (and men) to clarify this misperception. One woman anonymously revealed, "When I flirt with you, it means I like your company or find you fun to be with. It does not mean I want to have sex."

The law is gender neutral and a small number of women have been convicted of rape. The person who initiates and pursues sexual activity and who does the penetration is usually a man who risks being accused and cited as the perpetrator of rape.

Many programs stress improved communication as the key to preventing acquaintance rape. But emphasizing improved communication can miss an important point. Men's "communication" can do more harm than good, especially for women. Sexually aggressive men "communicate" to overwhelm women with continual pleas, arguments, and pressure for sexual activity. Victims of sexual assault clearly express their unwillingness by repeatedly saying "No," reasoning, physically struggling, pleading, crying, screaming, or freezing up when men's actions progress beyond their wishes.

The majority of women (nearly 70%) who survive sexual assault take some form of self protection during the crime (Greenfield, 1997 p.5). Nearly half of all rape survivors feared serious injury or death during their assault (Kilpatrick, D.G. et al, 1997, pp.844-5). There is a critical moment during an assault when a man knows that what he is doing is wrong and is violating the woman's will. Rapists act with a sense of entitlement and are clearly aware of their own actions, while disregarding their victims' objections and refusals. Sexually abusive men simply discount what a woman is saying or reinterpret it to fit what they want to hear. "When it comes to sexual relations saying 'no' is often meaningless when the words are spoken by a female" (Warshaw, p. 42).

Rapists commonly suppress their capacity to feel the pain of others (including victims), which diminishes a crucial inhibition against interpersonal violence (Lisak, 1996, p.723-726). They often ignore women's protests while employing verbal threats or using physical resistance (Lisak, 1996, p.739-740). Research reveals that many perpetrators believe that they were only "somewhat forceful" and admit to twisting a woman's arm or holding her down.

Male tactics of manipulation and force can occur when a sexually violent man becomes aware that his date/acquaintance is unwilling to have sex. Improved communication will not make a potential rapist more aware or receptive to a woman's requests. Portraying miscommunication as the critical tenet of prevention efforts can reinforce and perpetuate victim self-blame and offer men yet another excuse for their actions. "Her body language led me on," "She didn't say No," "She didn't really mean it when she said No," and "Hey, she invited me into her apartment," are excuses commonly heard during campus misconduct hearings. Behind these statements lies the fallacious assumption that the victim's communication and behavior caused the assault.

If men have been using alcohol and a sexual assault occurs, our culture allows them to feel less responsible – as well as to shift the blame to women if they have also chosen to drink. Regardless of their actions, women are not responsible for being raped.

Acquaintance rape survivors often question their own communication and refusal skills when they believe they were not clear enough in expressing themselves and hence were partially, if not completely, to blame for the assault. The betrayal of trust by an acquaintance, friend, classmate, or boyfriend, (in contrast with stranger rape), increases the likelihood of self-blame and causes a victim to search for the answers to, "Why did it happen to me?" or "What did I do to cause this?"

Men who commit rape often do not regard their actions as being rape. Considerable research shows that perpetrators of sexual assault are completely aware that their victims do not want to engage in sex. After analyzing his interviews of over eight hundred date/acquaintance rapists throughout the U.S., (the most comprehensive study of familiar rape), Stephen Thompson characterized them as being "egocentric, self-serving and manipulative" (Thompson, 2005). Male rapists do not handle rejection or criticism well. Many view women as sexual objects and believe they have the right to aggressively get what they want (rape) regardless of women's desires. Thompson also found that many perpetrators cunningly plan their assaults. Talk with any survivor of acquaintance rape (or read their story) and these characteristics and tactics are confirmed. Rapists control their victims with coercion, intimidation or force and expect submission to their demands.

Rape-prevention curricula must expose the dynamics of power and broaden our definitions of force, by revealing the tactics of control and manipulation that men commonly use during sexual assaults. Ben, a fraternity member from a Tennessee university frankly affirmed this point during an MVP program, "I think a workshop like this is good, (because) it's hard to discuss the fact that it [rape] might be in any of us." Raising awareness through education is the key. Encouragingly, when some men come to understand the law and see that their previous actions constituted rape, they feel remorseful and are motivated to change their behavior.

I work with men to improve their ability to "hear" women and clarify their misperceptions about the fallacious justification for using coercion and force. We examine the perceptions of viewing women as goals to conquer in dating relations and how boys are taught to initiate intimacy with a single-minded goal: sex. Regarding acquaintance rape as an impulsive act resulting from miscommunication is an over-stated myth that must be challenged and dispelled. Furthermore, focusing on communication detracts from our primary prevention work that explores men's beliefs, behaviors and personal responsibility. It also curtails the effectiveness of our programs for women (see chapter 10) that examine characteristics and tactics of sexually aggressive men. My definition of sexual assault is that rape is *never* the victim's fault and supports prevention educators and law enforcement/campus security who respond to these crimes.

I also address the facts regarding men who are themselves survivors of sexual assault, commonly in the form of childhood sexual abuse. When we recall the story from Chapter 4, "I was raped by two older neighbor boys when I was in the 5th grade. I was ashamed, confused and felt paralyzed for years afterward" we see more clearly how rape is more than 'just a women's issue.'

The next chapter explores a topic that is incorporated within my comprehensive MVP workshop: i.e., how peer pressure can influence the actions of male group members in horrific ways, such as gang rape.

SEVEN

Peer Pressure and Rape Prevention

What can an individual do to challenge the group?

The influence of peer groups on young men who are developing their sense of adult identity is continually evident in my work with fraternities, athletic teams, and boys who espouse an abusive ethos. Because peer groups can provide individuals with their primary sense of identity, members of male-only groups feel relentless pressure to conform to the values and mores of the group. Men's willingness to intervene in interpersonal violence can be influenced by group perceptions as well as their own. Men don't harass or rape a woman because of an inborn propensity, but can be motivated by a false courage that depends on their need for group approval.

Because peer groups can catalyze unconscionable behavior such as gang rape, men in fraternities and athletic teams are overrepresented among gang rape perpetrators (Gondolf, 1989). Members not only feel the need to impress other males – they fear being rejected and ostracized if they do not personify perceived group norms. In some instances, gang rape even represents an attempt to bond with peers!

Changing group culture begins with increasing the positive influence of individual members of the group. Since the majority of men are uncomfortable with violence against women, they can counter the negative attitudes and actions of abusive peers. My goal is to help men understand group influence and to encourage them to evaluate the costs and benefits of conforming to a group's values and behaviors. Although negative group dynamics fostered by a few participants (e.g., cavalier behavior, objectification of women and hypermasculine attitudes) can make facilitating MVP programs difficult, there are great leaders in every group whose benevolence has been constrained by peer pressure. My work creates a forum that empowers men to express their inner convictions and shifts group beliefs and values. As Tom, an Antioch College sophomore said during the conclusion of my mixed-gender workshop, "Yes men rape, and men can stop rape, including same-sex rape." Because of their stature in male social groups, this work increases men's ability to influence their peers-long after our discussions have ended.

My work with male groups begins with an introduction and overview of the workshop. I randomly assign them to small teams of four to five members to reduce large group influence, increase discussion time and reinforce the concept that all men (close friends or not) are uniting to stop rape.

An effective technique for developing men's prevention skills is to present a probable gang-rape scenario to small groups, who then brainstorm possible interventions. They explore the influence that peer pressure has on individuals to not confront sexual violence, and how that ratifies gang rape. I read the following scenario.

A Gang Rape Scenario

> You are at a crowded party (but not your party) with a few friends. There are kegs of beer and loud music, and everyone is drinking, dancing and having a good time. Late in the evening you notice four guys carrying a woman upstairs – a woman who is obviously intoxicated. You hear one of the guys remark, "She's passed out; time to get laid!"

My first step is to pose questions to the groups, including, "What are you thinking and feeling?" and "Why would it be difficult to do something in this situation?"

It is important to give men considerable time to discuss their feelings before moving on to the next step of creating interventions. Male socialization is often a barrier to the honest and open expression of feelings. Participants carefully examine the concerns that might inhibit their intervening. Men express fear for their own safety and believe that their intervention could lead to violence. They wonder aloud, "Is it worth the risk of having a fight for a woman that I don't even know?" Many express displeasure with the situation, yet feel unable to take action. They ask, "If I don't do anything, does that make me in any way responsible?" and, "What can I as an individual do to challenge the group?"

I welcome each of their concerns (feelings) as an avenue for them to gain insight into the difficulties associated with rape interventions. After ten to fifteen minutes of group discussions, I document their responses on large sheets of paper for all to see. It is paramount to examine first the difficulties to take action versus remaining a bystander in a situation. Then I explore the men's thoughts and their reasoning behind either their inaction or intervention.

I ask them to discuss how they could intervene using their intellect versus their brawn. I stress the power of using knowledge vs. physical force and humorously remind them that they are now in "higher" education.

I circulate through the room, observing their animated discussions. After ten to fifteen minutes, I ask each group to share its prevention ideas for all to hear. The strategies men create constantly inspire us all. I document them in bold writing. Peer-developed interventions have included the following:

* Shouting, "They're towing our cars!"

* Pulling a fire alarm.

* Calling 911 on their cell-phone.

* Pulling the plug on the loud music and pointing out the group to the entire party.

* Approaching the group and asking where they think they are going with your sister, your girlfriend, or a football coach's daughter (even if she is none of those.)

* Alerting the group leader, such as team captain or fraternity president, of the incident.

Others suggest asking a group of women to intervene; pointing out that a female group might reduce the likelihood of violence. Some men suggest telling the group that the woman has a sexually transmitted disease and discuss the unfair disgrace this assigns to the woman. Most men (and women) feel that it would be acceptable if it prevented a woman from being gang raped. Other men would confront the group, using force as a last ditch effort. I saw and felt the pride of these men as they shared imaginative and practical interventions with their peers.

I subsequently re-frame the scenario of the intoxicated woman's being "your friend, your girlfriend, or your sister." The men bristle at these suggestions and their faces often show anger. We discuss why men would undoubtedly risk taking immediate action if such were the case. I remind them that every woman is someone's friend, lover, or sister. Repeatedly, I have found that most men are disturbed by their peers' behavior in these devilish situations – but few have practical prevention skills. When men stand and describe their imagined interventions within a group, the impact can be profound and they challenge the norms of the group culture. They transform perplexing situations into concrete opportunities to stop male violence.

After a program's conclusion, I always leave the men's intervention tactics on large sheets of paper taped to the walls. This recognizes the participants' ingenuity and reinforces their commitment to stop violence against women. Men remember and can subsequently use their prevention strategies during their academic and personal lives because it was they who enthusiastically developed them. These skills can replace hesitation or inaction in future situations.

In part, my task as a male mentor is to model values and beliefs that do not support dominance or aggression. When I reveal my background as a college athlete my credibility is enhanced. As a former high school hockey player I am moved by the story of Sheldon Kennedy, which illustrates how any man is at risk for sexual violence (Board, 1997). Kennedy's story also validates how social pressure keeps men from acting to prevent and report sexual assault, thereby allowing abusers to continue to assault others. Kennedy, who played hockey for the Calgary Flames and Boston Bruins of the National Hockey League during the 1990s, was sexually abused for six years as a professional junior player by his coach, Graham James. To numb his feelings of shame and anger, Kennedy abused alcohol throughout his career before retiring.

Kennedy describes his teenage life as "…a lonely, living hell." His coach and "father figure" sexually abused him (once at gunpoint) while controlling both his hockey career and daily life from age fourteen to nineteen. Kennedy was unable to make friends, unable to trust, unable to love, and unable to feel "normal" unless he was drinking. Suicidal at times because of the inner turmoil that haunted him, he put up a shield: "I didn't let anybody in. It's a very lonely way to feel. You never feel normal." In January 1997, Coach James was sentenced to three and one-half years for abusing Kennedy and another unidentified player. Kennedy subsequently in-line skated across Canada to share his story; both to increase the visibility of male survivors of sexual abuse, and to raise money for a support center for victims of child abuse. This story reinforces the fact that rape is more than "just a women's issue" and that men are taking action against the culture that produces abusers.

Throughout my workshops and during informal conversations with participants, I display a lack of shame about being a man who embraces concepts of masculinity that are radically different from traditional ones. Although I believe deeply in our need to redefine harmful views of what it means to be a man, I also try to avoid being judgmental or condescending toward others who do not share my views. As long as participants are earnestly working with me I support and nurture their efforts, notwithstanding their mistakes. The unlearning of fifteen to twenty years of ideas about male gender roles is an ongoing process. One needs to be patient when helping men to walk the long path toward becoming a nonsexist male.

In summary, my workshops with men:

- Examine how peer pressure can be a catalyst for gang rape;
- Reveal that most men are uncomfortable with their peers' abusive behaviors;
- Establish that we can change group culture by increasing the positive influence of individuals in the group; and
- Authenticate that my male leadership approach can inspire peer-developed interventions in men's violence against women.

After two decades of prevention work I have learned how to create thriving groups of men who desire to reduce violence against women. Sustainable groups of Men Stopping Rape (MSR) can significantly change the peer culture that supports male violence against women. In the next chapter I share strategies for starting, framing, and sustaining a MSR group.

Sexual Aggression 101

A MVP workshop with student athletes

Photography by Mark Varadian

The Men's Violence Prevention Music Project

Terrance

Giles

Chris

Adrian

Photography by Mark Varadian

Gear Up with Music Students

Photography by Todd Denny

Men Who Stop Rape Are On Our Campus!

Many of us have girlfriends, sisters and mothers who have survived rape and domestic violence. All men (including faculty and staff) are invited to this workshop designed to create a Men Stopping Rape program on campus. Join with other men to end violence against women.

Date:

Time:

Location:

For more information contact:

EIGHT

Creating a Thriving "Men Stopping Rape" Group

Never underestimate the power and influence a small, active group of men can have on a campus or community.

IMAGINE WHAT IT WOULD BE LIKE if there were an active and visible Men Stopping Rape (MSR) group on your campus or in your community. What would it be like if rape and abuse were redefined as a man's issue rather than a woman's? How would your campus climate change if men took the lead in stopping violence against women? Over the years I have perfected tactics that keep men engaged and energized in prevention efforts. My strategies have been implemented by schools and colleges across the nation. I teach men the skills they need to positively transform their campus and community culture.

Men who are involved in ongoing MSR groups become better men as a result of their experience. Men not only fundamentally change their beliefs and behaviors toward women; they in turn mentor other men in their communities in life-affirming ways. MSR groups help young men to develop a sense of identity and camaraderie, similar to the experience of living in a fraternity or participating on an athletic team.

Recruiting men is not difficult with the right approach. Men who are ready to step up include athletes, fraternity members, high-school boys, musicians and students from every school and department on campus. Large campuses have hundreds if not thousands of men who are hungry for change and who are repulsed by male violence against women. Fortunately, there are men who have experienced training as volunteers working in crisis clinics and domestic violence/rape relief agencies. Unfortunately, few campuses create opportunities to help these men hone and increase their skills through MVP programs. Traditional violence-prevention programs rarely create the necessary passion in men who are available for the work at hand.

Inspiring men to remain involved is our task. When a campus takes the initiative to start an MSR group, early involvement may fade, not because the men lack interest, but due to the absence of innovative and important activity. In his landmark book, *Refusing to Be a Man,* John Stoltenberg (1990 p.134) emphasized the importance of action: "If we sit around and all we do is intellectual and emotional dithering, then we stay in the ranks of those who are passive enforcers of male supremacy."

There are approximately 3,000 colleges and universities across the United States. Fewer than thirty campuses have active, ongoing MSR programs that have existed more than two years. The following strategies can help you re-energize your MSR program or begin and *sustain* your high-school, community or campus program.

First, keep in mind that your goal is to create a thriving and sustaining MSR group – not to expend energy on a single, campus-wide event promoted with a lot of fanfare. Second, remember to take concentrated action on multiple fronts.

Consider using these tactics:

- Distribute flyers. Each week we leafleted the entire University of Illinois campus with MSR meeting flyers (See insert flyer: Men Who Stop Rape Are on Our Campus).

- Place eye-catching ads in your student newspaper.

- Set up an MSR booth for recruiting new members.

- Send out invitations to other men's groups and organizations.

- Develop a *succinct* and intriguing MSR recruitment presentation. Take it to residence halls, fraternities, athletic programs, and other campus organizations and events.

- Collaborate with campus women's groups who are serving as advocates and educators. Enlist their help – but *never* compete with, detract from or duplicate their efforts.

Continually evaluate the results of your actions. Have you created campus interest in your group that will attract potential members? Are you keeping those who are involved energized? Are you developing a solid core of men? (Note: ten active men are a strong base on which to build a MSR group.)

If you are not reaching your goal of creating a dynamic MSR group, make adjustments. Cultivate the art of flexibility. Be willing to acknowledge and change whatever actions have been unfruitful. Continue to make adjustments until you achieve your desired outcome. Find successful MSR programs and adapt their tactics to your campus. Sticking with a previously un-successful approach is a common pitfall. Be willing to discard it, think innovatively and take chances. Flexibility to make changes based on negative feedback is often an overlooked key to achieving success.

Work hard to enlist fraternities and athletic teams as "honorary" members. The president of the Interfraternity Council (IFC) at the University of Illinois became an important MSR member; and our collaboration subsequently developed into increased support from the 4,000 Greek men on campus. I was invited to be a liaison between IFC leaders and the Dean of Students, advising and coordinating IFC sexual assault policy and programming. This occurred by reaching out to the IFC and developing both formal and informal relationships. I took a pragmatic, outreach approach and refused to be chained to a specific model and encourage you to do the same. Each campus has its own nuances, strengths and men who are ready to respond to a creative opportunity.

Keep your MSR flyer simple and employ catchy graphics that fill the majority of the space. Resist the temptation to use trite, boring rhetoric that is indistinguishable from the language used in typical campus flyers, such as "A meeting will be held Wednesday evening for men who are interested in rape prevention." Instead, use intriguing graphics with a powerful message such as "Men Who Stop Rape *Are* on Our Campus!" Add, "To learn more...," and include the time, date and location of the meeting.

Students typically have busy academic and personal lives. It's important to find a scheduling "fit" for men to attend MSR meetings. Schedule your weekly, one-hour, lunchtime meetings at a central campus location. Most students eat lunch or have that hour available. Providing refreshments and food makes a difference.

When an academic department or organization offers you a meeting space, ipso facto they become an MSR cosponsor and ally. Use their support to build a strong relationship. At the University of Illinois, for example, the campus YMCA became our visible cosponsor after providing rooms in the heart of campus. Faculty clubs are also possible sources of places to meet.

Never schedule meetings on weekends and preferably not during the evening. I recall men expressing frustration and offering excuses for not attending evening meetings. And I remember sleepy-eyed guys on a Saturday morning who were uninspired by the prospect of spending a part of their weekend in another "class." We made the adjustment to hold weekday lunchtime meetings, and our core group grew from five to nearly twenty committed men, thereby stabilizing membership for the duration of the year. Never underestimate the power and influence that a small, active group of men can have on your campus and community.

A one-hour weekly meeting is sufficient to build a dynamic, ongoing MSR organization, two hours is too long and will deter progress and lower attendance. After your group is stable, a second hour can be used to plan and fine-tune your efforts in outreach education. If needed, enlist an experienced discussion facilitator.

Your initial meeting should be a "safe space" for members to meet and discuss their personal issues and reasons for involvement. Every member must be committed to confidentiality. MSR activity provides a common ground for members' ethics and interests, which in turn will foster cooperation and unity. Men will talk with one another more honestly if women are not present. Furthermore such frank discussions and revelations can be hurtful and revictimize women. We deconstruct our patriarchal ideas of masculinity by examining our own experiences and beliefs. The questions we analyze are more practical than theoretical.

Topics for group discussion might include:

* What attracted you to our group?
* How did we learn about sexism, racism, homophobia and violence against women?
* The messages and myths we have learned about being a man.
* The ways we have hurt women emotionally and physically.
* Examples of ways we have tried to rescue women.
* Discussions of men who mentored us in empowering ways.
* Discussing ways we have challenged or intervened in men's violence against women.
* Discussing how our lives would be different if there was no violence against women.
* Examinations of what kind of man we want to be with women.
* Discussing the kind of father you want to be with your children.

* Thoughts about how we can be allies with women.
* Developing collaborative partnerships with women's groups on and off campus.
* Developing a guiding MSR rationale.
* Activities we can take outside the MSR group on campus and in the community.

Profound conversations about difficult questions philosophically unify the group and reinforce its solidarity. Balancing group discussions with planned outreach activities helps sustain a successful MSR program. After a period of intense dialogue men need to see tangible results. The strengths of MSR groups lie not only with men connecting with other men but their experiencing the impact they can have outside the group. Discussing and unlearning sexism is the first step. Taking action to influence other men on campus and in the community is the second step.

Reserve the last half-hour of each meeting for planning your education events for the month and cooperatively assign tasks to group members. For example, if you decide to create a MSR outreach booth, determine who will:

* reserve the booth space;
* create and post promotional flyers for the event;
* create and submit newspaper ads to promote the event;

* create a MSR banner;
* develop informational handouts;
* man the booth for one-hour shifts;
* create a sign-up list for aspiring members;
* follow up leads to contact potential members;
* photograph the event;
* break down the booth; and
* write a follow-up article with pictures for the campus newspaper.

Activities such as distributing flyers, manning outreach booths, giving radio interviews, and protests build momentum by enacting program's goals and inspiring the participants to keep coming back. The intrigued and pleasantly surprised reactions on the faces of hundreds of students who visited our MSR booths at Illinois were a lasting source of inspiration and motivation for our group. Our outreach booths established a presence that touched the consciousness of thousands of students, shifted campus climate, and helped us recruit new members and allies.

The energizing activity of a creative protest gained national attention for our Illinois group. We learned from ads in our campus newspaper that Playboy magazine was visiting the University of Illinois campus for three days to recruit women for their "Women of the Big Ten" pictorial. Our MSR group agreed that at the very least Playboy is a major form of sex miseducation, and at worst it objectifies and contributes to violence against women. A woman in my coed program affirmed this point when she disclosed, "Pornography is a billion dollar industry supporting violence against women. It perpetuates the problem of sexual harassment, rape and prostitution by portraying woman simply as sexual objects that are to be used by men." We organized a one-hour, men-only, lunchtime protest in front of the hotel where Playboy had reserved a suite for the shoot. The Associated Press picked up our male-only protest, and the popular television show "Entertainment Tonight" interviewed us and aired our "Men Protest Playboy" story to millions of viewers.

Female allies of MSR called Playboy to schedule one-hour photo-shoot blocks of time and then did not appear for them. This tactic resulted in about half of the Playboy film sessions being unfulfilled with a consequent waste of the magazine's time and money. Playboy did not return to Illinois the following year. Such activities further energized our group, increased campus and national awareness, and inspired further education efforts. Without the consultation and support of women from other campus organizations and from our personal female friends, all this would not have been undertaken.

Our MSR group created an effective media campaign through our campus newspaper. We ran an educational series entitled, "The Rape Myth of The Week." Our ads consisted of eye-catching graphics with a statement that distinguished myth from fact. One was: "Myth: most rapes occur by strangers at night. Fact: most rapes occur between classmates, friends, dates, and co-workers." We included the tag line, "Want to learn more? Contact MSR at 333-1000." Our year-long, "Rape Myth of The Week" series increased campus-wide and community awareness of our group and produced calls of support from individuals and organizations. Our efforts enhanced a campus environment where women felt encouraged because men were displaying leadership in preventing rape.

While working in the Office of the Dean of Students, I was asked to create a brochure for men on the topic of rape. I tentatively titled it, "Men Must Stop Rape." True enough – but too bland! A revised title fed men's self-interest and intrigued them to read the brochure; it was, "Acquaintance Rape; How It Hurts Men" – again with eye-catching graphics. Requests for the brochure were so great that we reprinted thousands during the first year and throughout the next decade. Capitalizing on self-interest was the key to hooking thousands of young men to educate themselves about the effects of sexual assault.

Another far-reaching activity was our "I Pledge to Not Rape" media campaign. We recruited high-profile male student leaders in athletics, fraternities, and student government to affirm their commitment to MSR by having their picture taken signing a pledge. Our student newspaper featured their pictures in a weekly series titled "Men as Allies" (during April, "Sexual Assault Awareness Month.") A star quarterback and a fraternity president's public commitments to not rape can influence student perceptions and raise the visibility of male involvement dramatically.

To ensure group sustainability, send out a campus-wide email in the spring to male faculty and staff to identify potential advisors for your MSR group the following fall. Attach a brief, substantive statement about the principles that have guided your efforts and highlights of the year's activities.

Create strong campus-wide partnerships with campus professionals such as counselors, coaches, student advisors, campus security, and residence life staff. As members of your advisory group for example, campus professionals become stakeholders in your success.

Schedule a spring meeting for your fledgling advisory group to discuss activities to secure a continuing MSR campus presence the following fall. Specify actions and tasks for both the advisory group and MSR members and schedule a follow-up session in late summer to finalize plans prior to the start of the academic year. This gives your group a running start before the busy beginning days of the fall semester. Advisors and mentors will share and address common goals such as preventing the demise of your group due to graduation of its key student members. A strong advisory council of faculty/staff/community members also provides support during rocky times for your MSR.

Pay attention to a commonly overlooked fact – namely, that a new generation of students comes and leaves campus every few years. To ensure success, you must recruit new students and faculty/staff annually to replenish your MSR core group. Don't relax because your group is thriving; eventually your active leadership will leave campus. It's easier to recruit new members when you are on a roll.

Mentoring new members hones the skills of your current leadership and provides an influx of new energy, ideas and inspiration. Each successive group will retain its MSR history and have useful protocols to draw upon, thereby diminishing the unnecessary struggle to recreate itself completely.

In summary:

- A thriving MSR group can significantly change its participants and its campus/community culture.

* Every campus has many men who are willing to step up and get involved.

* Success comes from actions that capitalize on creative outreach.

* Develop innovative flyers and engaging approaches for outreach and education (See flyer insert: Men Who Stop Rape Are on This Campus.)

* Use the campus newspaper and website to tell your story and recruit new members.

* The ability of your MSR leadership to adapt and change approaches is a critical and commonly overlooked key to success.

* Look for other successful MSR groups for new ideas and possible strategies.

* Schedule efficient lunchtime meetings and be sure that your group talk is followed by actions on campus or in the community.

* Enlist faculty/staff/community members as advisors and mentors to ensure sustainability and to enhance your presence and political power on campus.

Each MSR group must develop its *own* guiding rationale. In the next chapter I present the rationale that underpins my work with men.

NINE

The Three Steps in Teaching Male Violence Prevention

Educators should not try to give men another set of beliefs – but help them understand how their beliefs can contribute to male violence.

My three-step programs for teaching men how to prevent violence against women:

1. Examine the beliefs men hold (see Chapters 4-7.)
2. Increase men's empathy for women victims, and
3. Teach men tactics needed for intervening and neutralizing in situations with high potential for sexual violence (see Chapters 5 and 7.)

Step 1. Examining the beliefs men hold. We first examine the values and learned behaviors that underlie men's violence against women. Educators should not try to *give* men another set of beliefs – but help them understand how their beliefs can contribute to male violence.

Attempts to reduce sexual assault through the education of women are not primary prevention and will not be successful until we also address directly the male violence that causes it. For example, we must examine the male belief that women who drink alcohol, or dress in a manner that men consider to be sexy or promiscuous, or are perceived to be sexually active, possess "deserving rape-victim characteristics." In my cross-gender programs I create opportunities for participants to challenge and clarify these and other male misperceptions about women. As a woman revealed anonymously on her index card, "If a woman is so drunk that she can't say No, then why would you interpret that as a Yes?"

By systematically addressing the false assumptions held by some men (and women) we can change the harmful behaviors that follow these assumptions – behaviors that pervade our culture and perpetuate male violence. Men's childhood experiences, home upbringing, and peer interactions can teach and reward patriarchal ideology. Secondary influences on men's beliefs include the media and popular culture. American boys grow up in a culture that condones and teaches aggressive behavior as part of the male status quo. Why is it that male violence such as school shootings occurs almost exclusively in the United States? Why do boys disproportionately represent the bullies, suspensions, and expulsions in our academic institutions? Why is it that 99% of all convicted rapists are men? Why is it that most perpetrators of domestic violence are men? I believe the answer lies with familial and social teaching that perpetuate male violence.

Why rape occurs is a fundamental question. Scholars who have researched this topic conclude there are multiple factors that increase the prevalence of sexual assault. Anthropologist Sanday

(1981) found that rape was either rare or nonexistent in a number of the 156 tribal societies she studied. She found differences in rape-free societies as compared with those in which rape was prevalent. Rape-free cultures were characterized by respect for women and sexual equality. Rape-prevalent cultures reinforced male dominance and high levels of male gender-based aggression and violence. Sanday concludes that men are not innately aggressive but that cultural conditions promote male sexual violence. Most rapists simply reinforce extreme societal forms of misogyny and anti-female values.

Lisak's research (1991) reveals how psychological and socio-cultural influences contribute to sexual violence. This includes differences in the types of relationships that rapist and non-rapist college students had with their fathers. Men who did not rape reported warm and close relationships with their fathers. Those who did rape had fathers who were emotionally and physically unavailable and in certain cases physically abusive. Lisak argues that distant father-childhood experiences, which he sees as being born out of our patriarchal society, create and teach harmful ideas about aggression and hostility toward women.

Sanday and Lisak's research helps explain why I have not addressed the question of biology in this book. Some researchers point to a vicious circle of mutual reinforcement between cultural norms that reward violence and the biological fact that men produce testosterone (which in animal studies clearly leads to aggression and violence). If this were true, the vast majority of men would be violent. My position is that violence is a learned behavior and can be unlearned when men understand the role of choice in their actions.

Step 2: Increasing men's empathy for women victims. I next facilitate an exercise that enhances men's empathy with women who have survived sexual assault. Placing men in the role of being a rape victim in a remedial empathy exercise increases their discomfort and defensiveness. Workshop participants must be permitted to choose their own levels of participation and not be manipulated in MVP education efforts.

At a national sexual assault conference, I attended a breakout workshop designed for male athletes. Facilitators from a prestigious eastern university described how they forced a male athlete to stand before his peers and play the role of a new inmate being groomed for prison rape. It was presented as a scare tactic to show men what happens to incarcerated rapists. The facilitators seemed pleased to describe how they selected a young athlete to be the rape victim. Although most conference participants appeared to accept the tactic, I refused to join them in their positive responses to the presentation and left the room. I remain critical of any approach that uses coercion. It is counterproductive to force men's participation in attempts to frighten them into not raping. What a sad irony: manipulation is at the heart of sexual assault and represents the very actions we are helping men to unlearn. Any coercive approach that forces men (or women) to participate in workshops does more harm then good. Coercion victimizes and embarrasses participants, and alienates them from participation, personal change and subsequent collaborative partnerships with men and women.

Nonmanipulative interventions enhance empathy for rape victims and can transform men's beliefs toward sexual violence. Showing men the shocking statistics on rape is useful but usually too impersonal and abstract to produce change in them. To comprehend something, we must do more than examine it intellectually. If we want to understand a person's traumatic experience (such as the experience of rape survivors) we must feel their feelings and emotionally experience something similar to the trauma.

The "Personal Traumatic Experience" (PTE) exercise we created at the University of Illinois in 1988 continues to be a life-changing intervention in my current MVP workshops. A poignant empathy experience occurred during my workshop for a large fraternity, many of whose members who were on a nationally ranked football team at the time. After I read a statement aloud from a confidential comment written by a participant, who described how he had been raped at the age of seven by two older neighborhood boys, a stunned silence ensued. Many were probably wondering which brother was the rape survivor and how this unimaginable act could have happened to a member of their fraternity. His personal revelation squelched latent, lighthearted attitudes and set the tone for the important work these men accomplished for the duration of the program. His experience revealed to the athletes how rape is not solely a women's issue and how it hurts millions of boys and men as well.

When I ask male participants in large groups to write anonymously about a traumatic experience in their lives, either recently or long ago, (something that scared or hurt them emotionally or physically) it personalizes the activity. Traumatic events harden our memory of the experience and the time and place in which they occurred; e.g., you probably can recall where you were when you learned of the 9/11 attacks.

I begin the PTE exercise by passing out index cards and asking the men to think of a time they had a traumatic family, childhood, or adult experience. Perhaps they were in an accident or were hurt physically or emotionally by a friend or stranger – any event that left them with a permanent hurt. I share a personal PTE experience to help them to reflect on their own. This reinforces their trust and exemplifies my workshop rule that I never ask a participant to do anything that I would feel uncomfortable doing myself. I allow time for the young men to contemplate and document their own PTE. This exercise sets an emotional tone and the room generally grows quiet and introspective. The confidentiality of writing anonymous cards in large groups provides men the safety they need to risk expressing themselves in personal ways. After they have written their PTE in a few sentences, I ask them to write briefly about their feelings and wants:

- How were they were feeling at the time, and
- The kind of response that would have helped them emotionally or benefited them during or after the incident.

I collect the PTE cards, shuffle them face down and read aloud several of the experiences. I create a thematic list of their associated feelings and wants on large sheets of paper and post them on the walls. Written memories, gleaned from participants on campuses across the nation, reveal poignant experiences:

- "My parents got divorced. Feelings: denial, confusion. Wants: someone to talk to."
- "Fraternity initiation. Feelings: confusion, weakness, anger, hatred and despair. Wants: I wanted out! Someone to tell me it was over."
- "My sister was raped when she was in high school. Feelings: anger, denial, shock. Wants: to be able to support her and take revenge on the assailant."

* "When I was younger my dad beat my sister unmercifully. Feelings: powerlessness, fright, anger, sadness. Wants: courage."

* "My girlfriend was sexually assaulted in her youth by a family member. Feelings: fear and anger. Wants: an apology from the assailant."

* "I watched my father die of a heart attack." Feelings: helpless, confused and scared. Wants: family, friends; and to turn back time."

* "I was hospitalized for six months for mental illness. Feelings: alone, hopeless. Wants: friendship."

* "My mom told me that for the past ten years she wanted to divorce my father, but she didn't because of me and my brother. Feelings: letdown, sadness, anger, worthlessness, suicidal. Wants: that it didn't happen."

* "My girlfriend's dad was beating his wife." Feelings: scared, pissed off, helpless. Wants: to have had some other guys there to stop him and for my girlfriend to have not been there."

* "When I was in second grade my neighbor made me have oral sex with him. Feelings: coercion. Wants: "Someone to have come home, because then I would have been all right."

From such statements, one can readily sense men's feelings of powerlessness, betrayal, physical pain, and fear of physical harm –feelings commonly associated with "rape trauma syndrome" experienced by women survivors. Feelings of female victims include helplessness, confusion, fear, isolation, hopelessness, and anger – the very ones that the men expressed.

Men's wants, much like their feelings, parallel those desired by female sexual assault victims. Female survivors wants include: someone to talk to, to turn back time, to have it not happen, to receive support of family and friends, to receive an apology from an assailant, for a trustworthy person to be there, and to receive justice. I present this exercise to reveal how traumatic experiences and associated feelings and wants are still clearly with men and how similar the feelings and wants are to those of female rape survivors.

We discuss how we can clearly remember these traumatic incidents, and their associated feelings and wants, even after ten, fifteen years or more. You can't say that about most of the events of our lives. The PTE opens the eyes and the hearts of men who haven't thought about the trauma and repercussions associated with sexual assault. For men who feel like rape is "not that big a problem," this approach can dispel that myth in a safe, personal way. The exercise also galvanizes the group's attention because of its candid nature.

For many young men in my workshops, this is a defining moment. This is the time when silence and introspection fuse with compassion for women who have been hurt by men. Some men enter my workshop embracing, "Is rape really a big deal? Move on with your life if you've been raped!" This empathy exercise enables them to see what a truly "big deal" rape is. They develop compassion for women survivors after having thoroughly examined traumatic experiences in their own lives in a safe way (many for the first time.)

I point out that the vast majority of the violence they described was committed by men against women, children, and other men – an obvious fact that comes as a revelation to some. Men discover that when they look carefully at their own lives, they can no longer blame victims. Because of their ability to develop compassion, which I find continually in almost all men, they come to understand the horrific carnage created by sexual violence. By accomplishing these first two steps of work, we achieve our goals of men's examining their beliefs and increasing their empathy for women – especially when working with groups of hyper-masculine athletes and fraternity members.

Step 3: Teaching men tactics needed for neutralizing and intervening in situations with high potential for sexual violence. We have already treated this important step in Chapters 5 and 7. To reiterate, my three-step approach to teaching men about violence prevention requires:

* First, that men examine their beliefs about women (and men as well);

* Second, for them to connect empathically with women who have survived sexual violence; and

* Third, for them to be guided in developing intervention tactics to neutralize violent situations.

Programs for women complement my primary prevention work for men and are explored in detail in the next chapter.

TEN

Enabling Women to Reduce Their Risk for Sexual Assault

Regardless of the situation,
no woman is ever to blame for her assault.

THE POSSIBILITY OF ACQUAINTANCE RAPE greatly affects women's abilities to develop trusting relationships with men. When women understand that the profile of a typical rapist is not that of a stranger, it follows that there are many men of whom women must be cautious, on-guard and wary. Preventing all male opportunity to rape is impossible, since we cannot eliminate all situations that place women at risk.

Male sexual violence occurs in a variety of environmental and social situations: about 40% of sexual assaults occur in the victim's residence; and approximately 20% occur in the home of a male friend, neighbor, or relative. Women's risk for assault increases when they are alone with men in isolated places. About ten percent of sexual assaults occur outdoors and about eight percent occur in parking garages (Greenfield, 1997, p.3). Place and environment are such broad concepts that it is difficult to describe a single scenario or situation that universally places women at risk.

But there are patterns. For example, we know that women have a much greater risk of being assaulted by a boyfriend, acquaintance, co-worker, or classmate than by a stranger. This seems counterintuitive because a lingering myth trumpeted by television and film is that rape usually occurs in unfamiliar places with strangers.

While it is true that environmental conditions can augment the likelihood of stranger assault – e.g., places with poor lighting, or when women have to walk due to inadequate public transportation – conditions which unfortunately have been the historical focus of prevention efforts. These issues must not be overlooked. Since stranger-rape accounts for only about 10% of all rapes, we must help women (and men) accept the fact that "ordinary guys" commit the majority of sexual assaults. There has been an increased awareness of the prevalence of acquaintance rape. But accepting the potential of a "typical" male to commit rape is too difficult for most women (and men) to acknowledge.

About half of the women who have survived acquaintance rape know they had a bad experience but do *not* define the event as rape. "Denial by the victim is rooted in the simple fact that she knows the attacker. If her assailant were a stranger, she'd have little difficulty in identifying what was happening. Instead she believes that if she just talks to the man and tries to dissuade him, he'll become reasonable. She searches frantically for some explanation of what the man's behavior means – any explanation that does not include calling what's happening *rape*" (Warshaw p. 54).

Freedom that men can take for granted is reduced significantly for women by the reality of rape. During my work at the University of Illinois we found that female students would stream out the central campus library to walk back to their residences before dusk, wary of traveling alone across a sprawling campus. The fear (and reality) of rape directly affected their academic opportunities. Women are warned not to walk alone at night – but what independent woman can actually adhere to that restriction and pursue her academic goals and social interests on campus? Many colleges address the issue of campus safety by offering rides home provided by student volunteers. The following incident illustrates that these risks exist for women *off-campus* as well.

Late on a beautiful summer afternoon I was jogging on a remote trail along a bluff on the edge of Spokane. As dusk slowly settled I found myself much further along the path than I had planned; I was confused about where to cut back to the road. I spotted a woman runner ahead of me who had stopped, and appeared to be taking in the spectacular view of the sunset. As I approached her I slowed to a walk and asked for directions. She acted as if I wasn't there and neither replied nor looked at me. I remember feeling annoyed and briefly thinking, "What a jerk"– but I sorted it out rather quickly. She didn't know me and was in a vulnerable position with a stranger in a remote area as nightfall approached. Recovering from my momentary pique, I moved on quickly to reduce her anxiety and eventually found the trail spur that led back to the road. It was a teachable moment for me. I know that I would feel trapped and be angry if I couldn't run or walk alone, when and wherever I wanted to. Were I in her position I would have done the same thing – and I just might have reached for my pepper spray! As a man I take for granted my freedom to run alone on a trail.

I turn now to my workshop that addresses prevention strategies women can use to sense, avoid or escape a potential rapist. This workshop was developed after facilitating numerous coed programs that attracted only women. My work with male-only and mixed-gender groups has also provided insights about approaches for working with women.

Workshops for women in tandem with those for men serve as precursors to mixed-gender sessions in a comprehensive campus rape prevention program. It's important to conduct single-sex workshops, however, to address gender-specific issues and fundamentally different learning objectives.

Fully eighty-two percent of rape survivors say that their assault permanently changed them (Warshaw, 1994, p.11). Anonymous comments contributed by female participants in my cross-gender workshops (discussed in detail in the next chapter) reveal both the feelings and ongoing challenges they experience:

> "The experience of rape is an emotion and fear that is passed on from generation to generation. This is one reason why female rape is thought about and feared so much by women."

> "Sexual assault might only last for a few minutes, but the pain, the hurt and suffering can last a lifetime."

> "I am in constant defense and doubt when I meet a guy. I am always fearful that no matter how nice they are they may hurt me."

More then half of all survivors of rape on college campuses were victimized during their K-12 years. A comprehensive examination in the state of Washington revealed that sexual violence is primarily an experience of childhood and adolescence, with eighty percent of victims reporting that their assaults occurred during their middle and high school years (Berliner 2001, p.53). Adult rape victims were primarily assaulted between the ages of eighteen to twenty-one years. Washington is regarded as a national leader in sexual assault prevention education, and its figures are congruent with the national averages.

The problem of rape is not only pandemic in American society, but common worldwide. Similar rates of incidence have been reported for several countries, with 19% to 28% of their college women reporting rape or attempted rape (Koss et al, 1994). Furthermore, research indicates that being a female survivor of childhood assault greatly increases the risk of adulthood revictimization on and off campus. Women survivors are at greater risk for rape revictimization than their non-abused peers.

Many otherwise competent educators and administrators are unaware of the vast number of women (and men) who began their middle/high school and college experience with the emotional and physical scars of a childhood sexual assault. Previous victimization also significantly influences women's academic success and social experiences on campus. Survivors on campus face a myriad of issues that accompany post-traumatic stress disorder from their assault: 30% contemplate suicide (Warshaw, 1994, p.66). They are 2.5 times more likely to abuse alcohol and drugs in their efforts to numb painful emotions and feelings (Resnick, Acierno & Kilpatrick, 1997). As a consequence, female survivors also have greater difficulty trusting men on campus and developing intimate relationships. They are at higher risk for academic failure and early withdrawal from school. Campus administrators must not overlook these consequences of sexual violence.

Rape survivors and nonvictimized women are usually mixed together in prevention programming without proper attention to their profoundly different life experiences. Education geared exclusively for so-called "typical" (nonabused) women should be redesigned to include components for previously victimized women. In my workshops that include men and women, I ask participants to stand silently if they know a survivor of rape or child abuse. The vast majority of female participants rise, along with many men. Programs for women should acknowledge and address previous victimization. For many women a workshop can provide them with their first opportunity to discuss their assault and begin the healing process. A campus rape survivor in a large California university reinforced this point, "When I first went in to see my counselor, it was like a huge weight was lifted off my shoulders."

The following description includes components of rape-prevention workshops for women that I have co-facilitated with women. Women also facilitate women-only programs without involving men, which can enhance honest dialogue and provide a greater sense of personal safety for female participants. Women typically take the lead in facilitating these programs, and involve men when appropriate. Enabling women to develop cognitive and physical self-defense skills are necessary components in a comprehensive rape prevention program.

We start by introducing ourselves and the program to the large group. We also briefly talk about why we are involved in rape prevention work. This continues to personalize the program and develops trust in the women who subsequently will be invited to share their life experiences.

We ask if there are specific issues or questions that the women wish to address during our interactive workshop, and record their questions for easy viewing by all the participants. These questions are subsequently addressed at appropriate points within the workshop format and during impromptu discussions. This personalizes the program, involves the participants, and assures that no specific needs are overlooked.

We acknowledge that discussing sexual violence can be difficult because:

* of our fears of sexual assault;
* we have family and friends who are survivors; and
* we know that some women in this program are likely to be survivors of sexual assault.

We encourage all to participate and assure them that, "If you choose not to speak, that's your prerogative. If you wish to take a time out at any point in this program, that's your right. And if you would like to talk with us after the workshop we will remain to do so." We also briefly share pertinent resource information about campus counselors, rape-prevention advocates and campus security.

We then provide an overview of the workshop's four key areas:

* Examining women's socialization in relationship to sexual violence;
* Examining characteristics of sexually aggressive men;
* Identifying at-risk situations, and developing personal avoidance/escape strategies for those situations;

* Defining sexual assault.

Woven into these topics are discussions and recommendations for how women can support their peers in at-risk situations and previously victimized survivors.

We break into small groups to provide ample time to discuss how cultural gender expectations hinder their safety. We randomly assign four or five participants to a group to foster the idea of all women as allies as well as to enhance new relationships. They discuss their experiences of "growing up female" and explore the connections between socially imposed gender roles and sexual violence. Through cultural conditioning, society can teach girls to be quiet, supportive and nondisruptive. Examining stereotyping of sex roles is important for both genders. Women who adhere to rigid gender roles increase the likelihood of their being victimized; and men increase the possibility they will perpetrate sexual violence (Lisak, D., Hopper, J. & Song, (1996).

We provide an opportunity for women to examine limiting and often harmful gender roles by asking them to discuss several of the following questions:

* What are the societal messages they heard and continue to hear about being female?

* What are the qualities our culture expects and values for our girls and women?

* What are the qualities our culture disapproves of and devalues for our girls and women?

* What is difficult about adhering to cultural expectations?

* What are the challenges associated with breaking out of these roles?

* What are the potential consequences for women who do not conform to these roles?

* How might culturally imposed gender roles increase women's risk for sexual assault and interpersonal violence?

After allowing considerable discussion time for these topics we move around the room, asking one woman from each group to share its key dialogue points, which we then document on the dry erase board. They discuss how as girls they received social approval by being nice and sociable and by pleasing others. They detail how they learned to put others needs first and to seek favor from men. Women discuss societal pressures to be polite, to not hurt others, and to be careful how they act and dress. They commonly acknowledge allowing men to take the lead in dating situations and how they are judged if they date several guys. Their topics all have implications for our prevention work.

We move on to identifying at-risk situations and avoidance strategies. The barriers women must overcome to achieve self-protection are often more cognitive than physical. Rape prevention must address women's tendencies not to trust their intuitions, their penchant for ignoring that "Oh-oh" feeling, their not wanting to "make a scene", and their not knowing the power of their own cognitive and physical strength. As one survivor anonymously disclosed, "What I learned from that horrible night was to trust my intuition." By encouraging women to examine their socialization history we help them to analyze it for those qualities that either hinder or help them in protecting themselves. Women can thus unlearn the cultural assumptions and practices that work against their emotional and physical health and safety.

By identifying high-risk situations and learning to trust their gut feelings when they are at-risk, women learn how to avoid male danger. Our goal is to help them understand that the risk for rape increases whenever they:

- are with an acquaintance of unknown trustworthiness;
- leave a social event with a man they don't know well;
- accept a ride from a casual acquaintance;
- date lots of different men;
- drink alcohol with men; and
- are isolated with a male (e.g., in a parked car, apartment, party, or fraternity/sorority house).

We remind them that if women go to a party or bar as a group, they should always leave as a group. The axiom is to "support your female peers by *never* permitting them to remain alone in high-risk social situations."

We next discuss characteristics of sexually aggressive and abusive men that include:

* Endorsing stereotypical qualities of masculinity and femininity.

* Trying to make women feel guilty if they resist unwanted sexual advances.

* Ignoring women's personal space/boundaries (including inappropriate touching, kissing, etc.)

* Ignoring, not listening to, talking over, and pretending not to hear women.

* Using alcohol/drugs as a tool to break down sexual reluctance.

* Having higher levels of aggression in general.

* Controlling women and espousing misogynistic beliefs.

We urge women to be on guard with men who display these behaviors, regardless of their charisma or attractiveness. A participant affirmed this point when she stated, "You can usually tell who you can and can't trust by their movements and their attitude. If a guy is aggressive right off the bat chances are greater that you'll have to worry about him." Another group of men fail to display these abusive qualities; they can be charming, cordial and polite until they attack. The vastly different profiles of rapists increase the prevention obstacles for women.

A rapist's success depends on setting up the situation out of earshot or view of other people. When a rape occurs in the victim's home, for example, the man usually knows that roommates, children and other adults are absent and he and the victim are likely to be undisturbed (Warshaw. p. 87).

Research also indicates that although rape survivors may sense the potential harm in dangerous situations they also tend to experience greater difficulty in acting on those feelings than do nonvictims (U. Texas-Austin, 1992). Designing a workshop that examines women survivors' heightened risks for revictimization would provide an often missing component in sexual assault prevention work. Research suggests that college-age women nurture their sense of identity through their relationships. They therefore may consider lack of connection with others as a lack of power. The strong need for connectedness can encourage women to be in high-risk situations (e.g., alone in apartments, dorm rooms, at parties and in bars with men of unknown trustworthiness).

Our next discussion activity examines the benefits and risks of women's needs for relationships. We ask the women to discuss several of the following questions:

- What are the benefits of developing new relationships with men?
- What are the risks of developing new relationships with men?
- What are social/dating situations that you have experienced or seen that might put women at risk for sexual assault?
- Why is risk increased in these situations?
- Did you have a gut feeling or instinct of the potential for risk in certain situations?

* Why is it difficult to act upon those feelings and assert yourself verbally or physically?

* What are the challenges in trying to get out of the situation?

* How could you act upon those feelings and get out of the situation?

* How have you acted upon your intuitive feelings and escaped a similar situation?

* How could you help and support other women in similar situations?

These discussions help women examine the dilemma of awarding their desire to avoid hurting men's feelings a higher priority than insuring their personal safety. Women, far more than men, are reared to believe that hurting others is wrong. Personal conflicts arise whenever a woman has to be candid, impolite, or assertive to reduce her risk of victimization. "No" is a sensible, powerful statement in and of itself – yet many women feel a "No" must be accompanied by a justifying explanation. We have our groups discuss and role-play how to avoid male assault by assertively stating their feelings, opinions, and desires.

Through acculturation and a focus on stranger rape, women can become habitual self-doubters in potential rape situations that progress until danger has accelerated to a clear and present form; when it is often too late to react successfully to prevent an assault. Developing the confidence and skills to risk embarrassment or awkwardness and thereby avoid or escape potential danger requires practice by all women in general, and is especially critical for survivors of sexual assault.

We next read the following scenario, "The Acquaintance" and ask them to place themselves in the situation.

> It was a Friday evening and I went out with a group of my friends to a club to hear a live band and go dancing. We ordered a round of drinks and had a great time unwinding, talking, and dancing. When I went up to the bar to get another drink I noticed a guy from my chemistry class doing the same. I thought he was cute and said "Hello." He recognized me and we had an animated discussion about the class and campus life. Mark was with a group of his male friends and they all joined our table for the rest of the evening. Everyone enjoyed the mix and we spent the evening talking, drinking and dancing.
>
> As the club was closing down, Mark asked if he could walk me back to my apartment. I was flattered by his offer and liked the idea of spending more personal time with him walking and talking outside of the noisy club. I told my friends I wouldn't need a ride home. When we reached my apartment there was a moment of awkwardness; he asked if he could come in for a nightcap. I was a bit hesitant, but he seemed like a nice guy so I agreed and invited him in. My roommate was out of town for the weekend so we had privacy to talk, which I enjoyed. After a drink and conversation he edged closer to me on the couch and started acting romantic and unexpectedly kissed me. I was totally surprised and caught off guard. He continued to kiss me more forcefully

> as I tried to pull away. He slowly began to unbutton my blouse as he was kissing me, telling me to relax. I felt scared and uncertain of what I could do.

We ask:

- What their reaction would be to the scenario.
- What are they thinking and feeling?
- What might happen if the woman tried to escape?

It is important to provide time for women to process their initial feelings and discuss their thoughts. Some women in similar situations have experienced hesitancy and have been unable to take action. They wonder, "What can I do?" We explore why women might feel unable to escape, and then document their thoughts and feelings by writing their comments on a dry erase board. Examples include:

> "Wow, he's coming on really strong and unexpectedly."
>
> "I'm shocked, I feel caught off guard."
>
> "He's buzzed from the alcohol, how can I stop his advances?"
>
> "I didn't expect this, how can I get him to stop."
>
> "He's pretty aggressive, I don't want to get hurt."

"I feel trapped."

"My roommate is gone and no help is available."

Our next step examines what, if anything, they could do to stop this from developing into a sexual assault. How could they confront, or speak out to Mark in a cognitive or physical way? The groups then evaluate the merits or pitfalls of potential actions. After ten to fifteen minutes of discussion time, we solicit each group's ideas and document them for all to view. Women's exit/escape interventions include the following examples:

- Shouting, "Stop. I don't want to do this."
- Assertively saying. "What do you think you are doing?" and forcefully pushing him back.
- Leaving with the excuse of getting a tampon and pulling the fire alarm (if available).
- Loudly stating, "What you are doing is a crime, stop it now!"
- Stating that you need to use the bathroom first and leaving the apartment or calling 911.
- Spilling your drink on him or the couch and quickly getting up "to get a towel" and exiting the apartment.
- Getting up with the excuse of more drinks or getting condoms and locking yourself in your room and calling 911.

A volunteer will then role play several escape tactics created by the women (while I re-create Mark's role), reinforcing the group's escape strategies in a more memorable way. We emphasize that each action is dependent upon the women's personal choice and safety – and that, regardless of the situation, *no woman is ever to blame for her assault.*

Women will also discuss their disinclination to accept Mark's nightcap proposal. They point out how mixing alcohol with a male of unknown trustworthiness augments their feeling of hesitancy and heightens their risk. Other groups state they would have declined his offer in the club, feeling it's too risky a situation. We affirm their intuition and acknowledge this is a primary prevention approach. Dalia, a California community college student summarized it well: "Whenever there is even a question of do or don't, back out of the situation, say no or just leave." Wendy, a New York private-college sophomore, said she'd "Talk her out of leaving the club with Mark by pointing out the risks", thereby reinforcing our concept of women as allies.

At this point in the workshop we discuss what legally constitutes rape (see Chapter 6). Most women and men do not label as rape those behaviors that meet the legal definition of sexual assault. For example, the use of alcohol to break down the sexual reluctance of a woman is an important consideration. Few understand that an intoxicated person is legally unable to give consent. We examine the prevalent tactics of coercion and manipulation used by rapists, and the role alcohol or drug use plays in the majority of sexual assaults. Coercion also includes talking someone into sex, as well as using verbal threats without being physically violent.

We clarify other forms of male coercion, such as using body weight to hold a person down and locking a door to prevent exit from a room. It is also important to discuss that women commonly become more intoxicated than do men (on the same amount of alcohol) because their bodies are generally smaller, and they tend to have less body fluid and more body fat than men. Because women also tend to have less alcohol dehydrogenase in their digestive tracts than men do, their bodies don't break down the ethanol as fast. We make the critical distinction that while alcohol does not cause sexual violence it *is* a contributing factor, increases risk, and *is* the primary rape drug in the U.S. The causes are the underpinning beliefs and behaviors that men hold toward women.

The program concludes with three prevention guidelines that we encourage women to embrace:

1. We reinforce the moral judgment that no woman is ever to blame for her being sexually assaulted, regardless of her dress, behavior, or actions. There is simply no excuse or justification for rape, in any situation.

2. We encourage women to increase their awareness of the effects that their socialization might have on their being in and escaping from potential assault situations. We remind them of their commitment to take action as an ally with an at-risk peer and to support women who are survivors of sexual violence.

3. We ask the women to trust their own intuition in high-risk situations and to get out, regardless of their hesitancy or feelings of awkwardness. Better a few moments of embarrassment than a lifetime of scars from a sexual assault. We encourage them to use the avoidance/escape strategies they developed in the workshop.

Women should receive whatever administrative support they need to be as safe as possible on campus. Violence prevention programs aimed at skill development should be part of campus orientation week or occur early in the school year. Campuses should also provide counseling, support groups, and other therapeutic services for all women and male survivors of rape and abuse.

Men who are committed to changing the culture of violence against women also deserve campus support. Women are encouraged by and supportive of MSR programs to empower men as anti-rape activists. They should be – their safety and lives may depend upon it. The next chapter describes how women and men can achieve more in this important quest by working together than they can separately.

E L E V E N

Men and Women Learning Together How to Stop Rape

Zero tolerance for men's violence
against women
can become a visible, expected norm.

Three-hundred first-year students sit pensively in their campus auditorium, waiting to hear a presentation on sexual assault. Some are nervous as they joke about the drudgery of date-rape presentations they suffered through in high school; they expect more of the same. Others sit silently, uncertain of what to expect from the anticipated "lecture." That they are not attending voluntarily further heightens their suspicion and anticipated boredom.

They are about to participate in Sexual Aggression 101 (SA 101), a program designed to inspire both men and women to explore and enact strategies for preventing interpersonal violence. My highly interactive presentation features music, lecture, and audience discussions about gender roles, alcohol and date-rape drugs, sexual assault, and men's role in prevention. It is imperative to introduce college students to the program in their first year, because freshmen tend to believe more rape myths than do seniors (Gray, Palileo & Johnson, 1993).

Women are at their highest risk for rape during their college years. In the course of a now-typical five-year career, one in five college women are raped (Karjane, H. M., Fisher, B. S., & Cullen, F. T. 2005, p.1). For a middle-sized college of 6,000 students with an even gender split, this means there will be about six hundred women whose lives will be forever changed by their sexual assault on campus.

By annually focusing on incoming student classes, we can reduce this chilling statistic and create a positive shift in campus climate and culture that will extend though their college experience and beyond.

Effective programming with college freshmen is critical, although ideally the work should begin in their middle or high-school years. Sexual violence is principally an experience of childhood and adolescence. Working with incoming classes over the course of four or five years can create a dramatic shift in a campus culture. Zero tolerance for men's violence against women can become a visible, expected norm.

Our grand opportunity is to help them examine the rarely discussed subject of sexual assault in an honest and empowering way. In mixed groups, men often dominate conversation. I remedy this by creating an environment where men listen to women expressing their feelings and beliefs. We can change the way students think and feel about sexual assault when we involve them in prevention. Students must be on the front line of all campus rape prevention.

I developed SA 101 soon after I created my music curriculum (see Chapter 3). We field-tested the program at four colleges and universities: independent audits of post-program evaluations certified the high participant approval of our approach. SA 101 continues to be extremely well-received in schools across the nation.

SA 101 opens immediately with a series of engaging songs that address racism, sexism, homophobia, alcohol and drugs, and sexual assault. By using musical metaphors and speaking to students in their own language, we both secure their attention and involve them in violence prevention (VP) efforts. Expecting a monotonous lecture, students are quickly intrigued by the music that carries our message. At the conclusion of the songs, I draw connections between their lyrics and the interconnected issues related to the sexual violence that affect their lives.

Students welcome programs that are interactive and not lecture-based. My work engages participants in candid discussions that examine the underpinnings of violence. The old adage, "Tell me and I'll forget; show me and I'll remember; or involve me and I'll understand" holds true for successful workers in the field of VP education.

Because of the sensitive nature of the topic of sexual assault, I explain that students should interact at their own comfort levels. No one is required to participate. I never force anyone to be part of an exercise with which he or she is uncomfortable. Our educational efforts should not be manipulative – a tactic that commonly underpins sexual assault.

I ask campus counselors, rape-prevention advocates, campus security and other helping professionals to stand and introduce themselves – and to briefly share campus resource information. It's important to personalize and put faces with the names of campus allies before the students' first week of instruction. Campus figures and the workshop facilitators remain after the program's conclusion to talk with students about feelings or issues that might have arisen during the workshop.

Next I present three issues that will frame our discussion by telling them what I intend to do; (and later I do it and conclude by reminding them what we have done) The three issues are:

* Why sexual assault occurs.

* What it is.

* What we can do to prevent it.

By guiding students through their life experiences chronologically I enable them to understand the underpinnings of gender-based violence. An introductory exercise helps participants reflect on the nature of cultural experiences that contribute to sexual aggression. I read a series of statements and ask students to stand up, silently, when a statement applies to them. Everyone has the right to stand or not as they choose. (Note: I sit in a chair and participate in this exercise. I assure them that I will not ask anyone to do anything that I would not feel comfortable doing.) What follows is the pattern of a typical Sexual Aggression 101 workshop.

I begin by reading,

"Please stand up if you would rather not be here."

Hundreds of students can be counted on to stand, thereby evoking laughter and relieving tension.

I commend them for their honesty and ask for this type of candor, along with respect for others, throughout our workshop. (Note: Never begin a program by asking students to discuss rape. Always give them time to warm up to the topic cognitively; then move into more sensitive, affective issues.)

I continue with, "Please stand up if you,

Are on scholarship: either academic or athletic."

(I ask those who stand if they would tell us the field of study or sport with which they are involved.)

have received a harassing phone call." (Women will outnumber the men.)

*have heard anti-female comments about women in your home, at school, or from friends at some point in your life."

(Most of the participants stand.)

When I ask for examples, a woman speaks,

"Everyday actions, small jokes and comments (about women) may seem insignificant, but they create a powerful, negative force."

Another woman proclaims,

> "We are people with hearts, spirits and minds. Think about us as a whole person."

Next I briefly discuss the connection between holding or espousing demeaning female beliefs and committing violence against women. Continuing on, I ask,

Have you ever felt pressure from friends to affirm your sexual prowess, or to boast about your successes?"

(I spark dialogue by sharing a personal experience about dating and peer pressure, which prompts students to contribute their own stories and experiences to the group discussion.)

> A male athlete stands to say, "In my high-school locker room talk about dating girls was always about who 'scored' and who didn't. I always felt pressure to do the same."

> A female student responds, "When guys brag about how many times they had sex and with whom they've had sex, it really makes me feel uncomfortable, and frankly it turns me off."

> A male student comments, "I feel that the images of both women and men in movies and TV can influence men to boast about their sexual conquests."

> A young woman states, "You guys are great, but don't be so influenced by other dudes. Even the most open-minded,

> strongest men seem to have real issues with how other men see them."

Continuing to facilitate peer education, I ask,

"Have you ever felt stereotyped, judged, or unfairly targeted as a male or female in our culture?"

(I offer a personal anecdote that encourages students to share their experiences of being mistreated because of their gender.)

Participants stand to offer their comments:

> A male student says, "I often feel stereotyped as a guy, even though I'm not a bad person."

> A woman adds, "Do not refer to women as ho's, bitches or chicks. We have names: use them!"

> A young man wonders, "Why am I made to feel guilty for my gender, when I have not assaulted anyone?"

I continue by asking participants to,

Stand if they know a survivor of rape or child abuse.

(A majority can be expected to stand.)

> A male student shares his story: "A friend of mine was raped in high school. It really shocked me."

> A confidential disclosure by a woman evoked emotion both in me and the student participants: "I've been raped, so I understand the fear a lot of women have."

After asking the contributors to sit down, I say, "Almost everyone knows or will know a survivor at some point in their lifetime." I prefer to use the term survivor instead of rape victim because it is more empowering for anonymous rape survivors who are participating in the workshop.

Next I ask,

> "Have you ever volunteered or worked at a rape relief/ domestic violence shelter or organization?"

(Several students will stand, usually women, occasionally men.)

I invite them to share with whom and where they worked and honor them for their commitment. The audience often applauds their work. I briefly tell my story and how it led me to my life's work.

A female volunteer declares,

> "When a woman has to enter a domestic violence shelter to heal from physical or sexual abuse, it disrupts and changes her world to a degree that most people cannot imagine."

My next step is to ask,

> "Has anyone ever done something to stop sexual aggression?"

This question commonly elicits responses from the young men in the audience. They describe intervening in situations where women were at high risk for sexual assault.

For example, a young man frankly detailed his intervention in a likely rape situation. An intoxicated woman at a party had been targeted by another guy for sexual coercion (rape) because of her vulnerable condition. He confronted the aggressive guy and offered the woman his assistance. After he sat back into his seat, the audience (as so often happens) applauded his effort.

These stories captivate the students' attention and validate men's roles as being in solidarity with women. For many in the audience, it is their first experience hearing men discuss the need for male leadership in stopping sexual violence.

It is important to redefine rape prevention as a man's issue, too. We tend to think of sexual violence exclusively as a "women's issue." But it affects both genders: our lives are intertwined, and at some point a woman (or man), who is close to us, will either disclose a previous assault to us or themselves become a survivor of rape.

A young man verifies my point with his story: "A friend of mine was raped her first year in college. I didn't know what to do or how I could help her." The group silently reflected on his disclosure.

In the next exercise, I read a variety of unfinished statements designed to prompt further student involvement. (Note: for smaller groups I post these on the walls around the room.) I ask students to use their own voice to finish any statement they might feel comfortable to discuss, and again assure them that no one will be pressured to talk. Moving around the room, I facilitate participants' animated opinions about the beliefs that underpin sexual aggression.

Examples of participants' responses to unfinished statements follow.

When I read,

"An awkward thing about dating is…"

> A young woman comments, "It seems that men and women perceive body language completely differently."
>
> A male says, "It would be easier if women would say what they want you to know and not expect you to sense it."
>
> A woman adds, "It's awkward trying to understand what men really want and need from an intimate relationship."

Another prompt begins with,

"I can tell someone wants to be kissed when…"

> A woman shares, "I think it's cool when a guy asks if it's OK."

Men's common responses include

> "I can tell by her body language."
>
> "It's just a feeling that I have."
>
> "I can see it in her eyes."

I discuss how these non-verbal cues and assumptions can be replaced with; "May I kiss you?" or, "Would you feel OK if I kissed you?" Verbal consent is an important element of all intimate experiences, because sex without consent increases the likelihood of rape. Freedom to choose includes saying "No" or stopping at any point. Choice guards mutual safety and enhances respect.

Another probe starts with, "If a woman drinks…"

A woman asks a penetrating question of the men in the program,

> "How drunk would a girl have to be for you guys to take advantage of her?"
>
> A male adds, "Although there is never an excuse for rape, both men and women need to be pragmatic about their behavior – for example how much we drink, our clothing, and sexual behavior."
>
> Another woman comments, "If you have to use alcohol to get a girl, then you're not a man."

I remind the workshop participants that some men stereotype a woman who drinks alcohol as being a "deserving rape victim."

Next I read,

"Men's responsibility for sexual aggression includes…"

A man comments, “When a woman says “No”, it doesn’t matter how it was said, all us guys must understand that it means No – or else there is a violation happening.”

Another male adds, “As men, we cannot rescue women, all we can do is stand up for our own beliefs about rape when dealing with other men.”

Another unfinished statement that elicits thoughtful responses is,

“Women’s responsibility for sexual aggression includes…”

A woman responds, “Trying always to stay in groups and knowing that there are guys out there who might take advantage of you.”

A second woman observes,

“Communication. I’m not sure either gender knows what the other is saying most of the time.”

Sure-fire statements to encourage student participation are:

“One thing I hear about fraternity men on this campus is…”

“One thing I hear about sorority women on this campus is…”

“One thing I hear about male athletes on this campus is…”

> "One thing I hear about female athletes on this campus is..."

Responses to such statements vary from one campus to another but are sure to be provocative. Students' comments can reveal subtle characteristics of campus culture and hints about campus violence prevention needs.

Upon hearing,

> "One thing that would help prevention efforts on this campus is..."

A male student eloquently comments,

> "I think men need a forum to talk about the fact that we are the ones who perpetuate most of the violence. This reality affects our psyche."

I continue our conversation with,

"I feel manipulated in a dating situation when..."

> A female responds, "When I'm with a guy who is too sure of himself."
>
> A male responds, "When I get mixed signals from a woman I'm interested in."

> Another female adds, "When I'm with someone whose verbal style is to interrupt, to speak first and thereby silence me."

When I read, "Women who wear sexy clothes…"

> A woman comments, "I would like to wear something sexy without hearing a sexual remark. If my clothes show my skin, it doesn't mean I'm easy."

> Another woman adds, "What I wear has nothing to do with you getting laid."

I continue reading, "If a woman goes back to a guy's room."

> A male forthrightly responds, "Most guys would assume that something (sexual) is going to happen!"

> Another male adds, "I think a guy would think a girl was absolutely nuts if she said to him, 'I'll go to your room – but not to have sex.' What does she think should happen?"

> A woman's anonymous comment balances the previous views, "Let us initiate. We don't always look for sex."

Such comments quickly produce clarifying responses from women who address men's questions, assumptions and misperceptions.

When I pose the statement,

"My sex education came from …"

> most students will say that their sex education came from their peers and friends.
>
> Less than a third will say they received practical or memorable education about their sexuality in school or from their parents. We discuss how the majority of our "sex education" turned out to be half-truths or faulty information.

At this point in the workshop, previously silent students feel increasingly comfortable to speak with their peers. I have found this to be true even with a group as large as two thousand students! The power of this program lies with creating a "safe space" for dialogue by first navigating through the chronology of life experiences that have influenced students' beliefs about gender roles, dating, communication, and sexual assault. I sequentially and non-threateningly create opportunities for students' voices to be heard on progressively difficult issues.

Curious eyes watch and voices grow silent when a first-year student stands and speaks. Peer education is compelling and can capture an entire group. I acknowledge that I certainly would not have had the courage to speak up when I began college. As any skillful workshop facilitator would, I validate participants' contributions and distinguish facts from myths. These exercises both set a tone for involvement and trust and acquaint me with the group's values.

Building on their personal experiences and beliefs, I next examine the connection between sexual aggression and culturally imposed roles for men and women. This exercise is important because students who adhere to rigid gender roles increase their likelihood of being involved in interpersonal violence. Sex role stereotypes limit emotional expression and the ability to behave as honestly as one desires.

I delve into stereotypical assumptions about men being strong, powerful, sexually-promiscuous, domineering and in control of dating situations. I add that our culture encourages men to take the lead in dating, while it teaches women to be unassertive, quiet and non-disruptive and to not make a "scene" if a date evolves into a high-risk situation (Lisak et al, 1996). These statements provide a lively forum for participants to express their discomfort or support for these limiting and too-often harmful expectations of men and women.

I pose several of the following questions:

* Who puts us in these roles?

* What's the hardest thing about adhering to these roles?

* How might these roles contribute to violence against women?

* How might they contribute to women's being at risk for sexual and domestic violence?

* How could they contribute to men being perpetrators of sexual assault and domestic violence?

* How might these roles limit men's abilities to prevent sexual assault?

I document the answers from their conversations on dry erase boards and periodically review and highlight their key points. Students often voice opinions about alternatives to normative expectations of women and men. Discussing honest feelings and beliefs about living life free of cultural constraints helps to balance harmful assumptions. These discussions prepare students to develop intervention skills and compassion for sexual assault victims.

The next stage of my workshop introduces facts about sexual assault. Illustrative statistics (O'Sullivan 1991) about acquaintance rape include:

* One-quarter of women will be victims of rape or attempted rape.

* Most victims do not report the crime to officials.

* First-year college women are at greatest risk of sexual assault. The first quarter/semester is the riskiest time.

* Alcohol, although not the cause, is a factor in about 75% of acquaintance rapes.

* Many rapes occur with a male acquaintance in isolated places, e.g., an apartment, dorm room or parked car.

* Many women and men don't know what legally constitutes acquaintance rape.

I present the above statistics to confirm the widespread prevalence of campus rape. In the mid-eighties, Ms. Magazine reported findings from their survey of over 7,000 students in thirty-five schools (Koss, 1988). The "Ms. Magazine Campus Project on Sexual Assault" is still the largest study of its kind and its findings have been extended and corroborated by recent research (Koss, 1994, Tjaden & Thoennes 2000, 2006).

I ask participants,

Why do you think a first-year woman on this campus would be at greater risk for sexual violence than a junior or senior? Individuals stand to provide answers:

> "She might be more naïve about campus safety."
>
> "It's her first experience with total freedom from home life – free to drink and party as she pleases."
>
> "She might be coming from a safe home environment and be unaware of the potential dangers on campus."
>
> "Some upper class-men target first-year women as being easier for sex."
>
> "She might feel pressure to fit in and develop friendships, even with guys she doesn't know too well."

I extend the students' thinking by asking why the riskiest time for campus rape is during the first term. Students discuss how the first semester is traditionally a time of social gatherings, partying, and meeting new people. They invariably corroborate the research findings that alcohol is their drug of choice in these mixers. Participants continually provide their own answers to many issues that I want them to address. By engaging them with their ideas and placing them in a leadership role, I am able to "capture" students for the program and nurture peer leadership.

Next I reinforce how women are at increased risk for acquaintance rape when they are with men of unknown trustworthiness in isolated places; e.g., in an apartment, dorm room, parked car or at a party secluded from others. Some might claim that I'm anti-male when I facilitate such a discussion – but I'm simply being honest. This baseline of information helps our prevention efforts become gender specific and more relevant. Facts must be discussed in an honest, non-accusatory manner (another important workshop guideline).

Addressing the relationship of alcohol and sexual violence, I clarify that alcohol does not cause rape. The causes of sexual violence are the beliefs and behaviors that we are discussing in the workshop. Alcohol is certainly a contributing factor and is commonly used as the excuse for rape: "I was drunk," "We were drinking," "I had beer goggles on," and "She lead me on," etc. When students tell me they drink to loosen their social inhibitions and to relax, I remind them that they make a choice to do so. I present more specifics on alcohol/drugs during the "redefining rape" section of the workshop.

I then discuss three of the so-called deserving-rape-victim characteristics that some men (and women) in our culture embrace including:

* She has been drinking.

* She is dressed in a way that guys might consider sexy or promiscuous.

* She has more than one boyfriend or is perceived to be sexually active.

Women's anonymous index-card responses on these topics illustrate both insightful and contrasting views. Two follow:

> "Don't assume that, just because I drink and dance with you that I'm interested in pursuing a romantic relationship with you."

> "I'm tired of a woman being labeled a 'slut' or a 'whore,' whereas a man with just as many partners (if not more) is called 'the man' [or a stud] and is congratulated and praised."

I affirm the women's statements by leading an exploration of how men can exhibit the same actions as women without the fear of receiving harsh social judgment or the risk of being sexually assaulted.

I then discuss the legal definition of sexual assault (see Chapter 6).

My final exercise allows every participant to share safely her/his thoughts and unspoken feelings regarding their workshop experience. I ask them to write a brief, anonymous message to the other gender on an index card, regarding something they would like to explain; or to express something they feel the other gender does not understand. I suggest that it can be about dating, communication, gender roles, misperceptions, or another issue that resonates with them and the goals and purposes of the workshop. Students quietly contemplate and write summary statements about their program experiences. After about five minutes we collect the cards and sort them by gender.

Four pre-selected student volunteers (two men and two women) take turns reading the cards, while their peers listen attentively. Women's statements include:

> "Hesitation on a woman's part is a red flag that things are not okay. Don't assume this is just her silly fear."

> "I'd like you to know that you men seem strongest when you are willing to be vulnerable and open about your fears and feelings."

> "A woman doesn't have to explain or give excuses when she doesn't feel comfortable doing something. If your partner won't accept your wishes he isn't accepting you and you don't have to take that."

> "How would I go about letting a guy know in a polite way that I do not want to have sex with him – so he would still interested in me? What can I do to show a guy that I am interested in him without his thinking that I want to have sex with him?"

> "If I like to get out and party, if I like to talk about sex, it doesn't mean that I am easy."

> "A soft, polite and kind 'no' still means **NO**!"

> "I think you guys are beautiful and interesting. This makes us want to be with you, but only by mutual acceptance. Anything taken by force is no longer beautiful."

These rich, personal statements from female participants provide a workshop facilitator with grist for her/his peer-education mill. More importantly, they provide relevant information for the students themselves.

Two male volunteers then read the men's statements, which include the following:

> "The rape victim is never to blame. Do not allow patriarchy to make you feel bad about yourself."
>
> "No is a respectable answer for a woman to tell a guy, anytime."
>
> "I want to learn how to trust more and be a better man."
>
> "I think it is unfair that women are restricted in their freedom because of the possibility of sexual assault."
>
> "As I grow to know myself more completely, I hope my partner and I can come together in ways that affirm each of us as a gift to each other."

Students' insightful statements reflect the work that they accomplished during a workshop that was meaningful for them. Their thoughtful quotes arose within a program characterized by an examination of real-life issues related to sexual violence. For many students the safety of writing anonymously on index cards allows them to express themselves in a way that would be awkward in a large-group setting. This inspiring, closing exercise provides another opportunity for each student's voice to be heard and honored.

Participants in SA 101 examine personal issues that are more profound than mere facts about male violence presented by a facilitator. Rather, men and women share incidents from their lives and experience the power of collaborative partnerships. My workshop galvanizes the group's attention because of its candid and personal content. The program concludes by affirming the approaches to rape prevention that students discussed.

* First, I encourage them to continue to educate themselves and compliment them on being a select group that now has increased understanding about campus sexual assault. I stress the power of their continuing their conversations outside the workshop. Since they all know and talk with at least 3 people on campus, in a group of 300 that extrapolates to 900 people who will learn more about campus rape!

* Second, I remind the students of the importance of redefining force in terms of coercion and manipulation, and the need to understand the role that alcohol/drug use plays in the majority of sexual assaults. I reinforce the principle that coercion can include talking someone into sex, using alcohol as a tool to break down sexual reluctance, using body weight to hold a person down, or locking a door to prevent exit from a room.

* Third, I strongly encourage men to continue to take an active stance against sexual aggression throughout their collegiate lives. I ask them to take a risk and challenge, confront, or speak out against men's violence against women.

Female students often approach me after a program to discuss their victimization or that of a friend or family member. Illustrative of their poignant stories is Dana's statement, "Rape is not a one-time act. It stays in the rape survivor's mind and heart forever. It affects who we date, who we look at, and what we accept. It replays in our minds." Dana summarized the horrific truth of being a rape survivor.

I urge campus faculty and staff to hold discussions with all students, both new and those returning to their campus, on the issues that we have explored; and gently remind them to engage students, not lecture them.

TWELVE

Conclusion

It takes a community of men to stop rape.

I OFFER THIS BOOK AS A "HOW-TO" GUIDE for those who wish to begin, enrich and sustain needed conversations and activities to prevent male violence. These exercises, engagement techniques and students' comments were gathered during twenty years of my work with students in higher education, public schools, and other institutional settings. Principally, I seek to teach young men the skills they need in order to examine, unlearn, and how to work to change the patterns of male violence. My violence prevention programs grew out of academic training, experiments, trial and error, and from planned and unexpected program successes.

The power of storytelling as a pedagogical tool helps deliver and refine my message of men's violence prevention. I encourage participants in my workshops to tell their stories which I combine with evaluative data to improve my interventions. The comments that participants make during and after their workshop experiences inform me about the merit of my programs. I use their formal and informal comments to both alert me to necessary program changes and affirm program strengths. When students share their life stories during my workshops, their peers listen with rapt interest. When students tell or write about how MVP programs have made a difference in their lives, I share their stories in subsequent programs.

With each passing year, I feel more strongly that there are no social programs we should nurture more lovingly than those advanced by our sexual assault/domestic violence advocates and prevention educators. Those who are dedicated to breaking the cycle of violence and planting seeds of peace within our cultural consciousness are among our most important leaders for societal change. Future generations will build on their rich traditions. The current teachings now being passed on by thousands of female educators will continue to attract men as allies in the movement. By legitimizing and sustaining MVP education, succeeding generations of men will develop skills to overcome personal and institutionalized acceptance of sexual violence and abuse.

I see two kinds of participation in MVP. The first includes vocal support and expressions of willingness to help. When a man donates money to a community sexual assault/domestic violence provider, he shows his willingness to support advocacy for abuse survivors. But his gift does not necessarily mean that the donor practices nonviolence. The second kind of participation in MVP is one of active and transformative learning. Personal and social change is accomplished only when men practice what they proclaim.

To make significant inroads in reversing male violence, we must look beyond the obvious problems associated with the men who abuse women; we must examine the flaws in a society that has produced far too many perpetrators of such crimes. How we address issues of male violence against women reinforces our own values (consciously held or not) and determines the depth of our interventions and opportunities to realize unprecedented social change. Our work must help young men change misinformed concepts of masculinity, shaped by family and culture. We must also transform our hopes into action.

In his beautiful book, *Peace Is Every Step*, Thich Nhat Hanh (1991, p.41) – a Vietnamese Buddhist monk whom Martin Luther King, Jr. nominated for the Nobel Peace prize – describes hope as an obstacle: "When I think deeply about the nature of hope, I see something tragic. When we cling to our hope for the future, we do not focus our energies and capabilities on the present moment." I, too, have found hope can be a passive and formidable barrier to the actions we must now take to engage men in violence prevention.

There have always been men in our society who are ready to accept the challenges created by male violence against women. Such men are now present in great numbers. If we don't help them, who will? Men can and must help women shed the false burden of responsibility for rape, domestic violence, and abuse. I say "false" because it is men who overwhelmingly rape and abuse; and it is men who must stop it. We must think critically about our values, beliefs, and approaches in our work with men and make the very changes in ourselves that we ask of them. By working compassionately with men and having an expectation that they will respond positively, we can and will achieve justice.

It takes a community of men to stop rape.

Acknowledgments

David Whitener: you put me on this path and I thank you. Fred Schrumpf and Golie Jansen: you continue to be two of my greatest teachers. Golie's brilliant editorial and structural comments significantly enhanced this project. My father, Terry Denny and Tim Wallace: your editing and personal encouragements throughout the development of this book were incredibly helpful.

Chandra Lindeman's warm support and insightful feedback improved the quality of this book; and JeniJoy LaBelle's comments refined the style of my stories. My personal friends Jon Holz, Francis Hearn and Jeff Allen reviewed and commented on the manuscript and offered helpful ideas and inspiration. Sam Weintraub, Brian Mustain and John Dougherty's help on initial drafts increased the quality of this book.

Among the many women who helped me at Safeplace during my internship I am most thankful for Charlotte, Tonya and Ann, who took the time to support me during my challenging first few years in 1984-85. Were it not for them, I might have dropped out of the training process. I was also fortunate to have three talented male mentors at Safeplace: Daniel, Steve, and Garth taught me the possibilities for men's involvement in working with survivors of both sexual assault and domestic violence. Tom Nogler was another important male teacher. Men's involvement was rare then, and remain so today in most rape relief/domestic violence shelters.

I am indebted to Mary Ellen O'Shaughnessey at the University of Illinois for her outstanding mentoring in violence prevention and advocacy and to John Stoltenberg for his wisdom and support of my work. I express my gratitude to Mark Varadian for skillful photography, web design and word copy. Thank you Paul and Patty Richards, Michelle West, Shianna and Lisa C at the Sente Center, for their impact on my life and work. Debi Bodett and Bonnie Zielinski: your imaginative MVP graphics design was just what I needed.

To all the men who volunteered with the Men's Violence Prevention Music project including; Chris Sand, Gile's O'Dell, Adrian Madrone and Terrance, you were magnificent. My deep appreciation for the efforts of Khalil Islam and Carol Vines at Eastern Washington University, Eileen Dunn at Green River Community College, Steve Thompson at Central Michigan University, Men Can Stop Rape including Patrick Lemmon and Pat McGann, Men Stopping Violence, Atlanta, Georgia, the Oakland Men's Project and Men Stopping Rape, Madison, Wisconsin. The Olympia, Spokane and Tacoma School Districts all provided support for my programs.

Thanks to Jan and Nan LaBell, David Hellstrom at the Bacchus network; to Matt Grant, principal of Olympia High School, Mukti Khanna, Elizabeth She, Luc Burson, Minerva Garza Everhart, Peter Epperson, Darcy Lees, Beth Reese at the Safe Schools Coalition, Alan Berkowitz, Gayle Stringer, Norm Nickles, Rosalinda Noriega, Mary Craven and Nalini Nadakarni; you all lent a helping hand.

The Evergreen State College, Dalia Gomez, Mickey Newberry at the Washington Attorney General's Office, Washington Governor Christine Gregiore, Washington Senator Lisa Brown, Bob

Stake and Bill Riley Dean of Students at the University of Illinois, Heidi Stout, Chu Usadel and The Timberland regional library provided needed assistance.

Stafford Hood, Golie Jansen, L.T. Wallace, Chandra Lindamen, Senator Lisa Brown, Guy Sensese, Theresa Schinzel, Fred Schrumpf, Sam Weintraub and Charles Prickett: your warm reviews of my book were a pleasant if undeserved surprise.

I thank my parents for raising me to be who I am and for their thoughtful comments and suggestions on my work over the years.

My fondest thanks go to the men and women who participated in my workshops and trainings over the past two decades. It was you who provided the stories which helped bring this book to life and are my inspiration to continue the quest.

References

American Academy of Pediatrics (1994). Sexual assault and the adolescent. Retrieved December 2, 2006 from *Pediatrics*, 761-765, Retrieved December 20, 2006 from web site: **http://www.aap.org/**.

Berkowitz, A. (2003). Applications of social norms theory to other health and social justice issues. In Perkins, H.W., (Ed.). *The Social Norms Approach to Preventing School and College Age Substance Abuse: A Handbook for Educators, Counselors, Clinicians.* San Francisco: Jossey-Bass, 259-279.

Berliner, L. (November, 2001). Sexual assault experiences and perceptions of community response to sexual assault: A survey of Washington state women. Seattle, WA: Harbor View Medical Center.

Board, M. (1997, Jan. 7). Abuse case wake-up call for hockey: Sports psychologist urges prevention through education. Alberta, Canada: *Calgary Herald.* p. C.1.

Collins, K. S., Schoen, C. & Joseph, S. (1999). Health concerns across a woman's lifespan: A 1998 survey of women's health. New York: The Commonwealth Fund. Retrieved December 2, 2006 from web site: **http://www.cmwf.org/**.

Denny, T. (2003). Dating violence teaching module in the teen dating violence curriculum, protecting our children, "Hands" music video. WA State Attorney General. Retrieved from www.todddennymvp.com

Gondolf, E. W. (1989). *Man Against Woman: What Every Woman Should Know about Violent Men.* Woodmere NY: Sulzberger & Graham Pub Co.

Gray, N. B., Palileo, G. J. & Johnson, G. D. (1993). Explaining rape victim blame: A test of attribution theory. *Sociological Spectrum*, 13, 377-392.

Greenfield, L. A. (1997). Sex offenses and offenders: an analysis of data on rape and sexual assault. Washington D.C: Bureau of Justice Statistics, U.S. Department of Justice, 39 pages.

Karjane, H. M., Fisher, B. S., & Cullen, F. T. (2005). Sexual assault on campus: What colleges and universities are doing about it. Washington D.C: U.S. Dept. of Justice, National Institute of Justice, NCJ 205521, 18 pages.

Kilpatrick, D. G., Edmunds, C.N. & Seymour, A.K. (1992). *Rape in America: A Report to the Nation.* Washington D.C: National Victim Center, SRS104, 16 pages.

Kilpatrick, D.G., Acierno, R., Resnick, H.S., Saunders, B. E. & Best, C.L. (1997). A 2-year, longitudinal analysis of the relationships between violent assault and substance use in women. *Journal of Consulting and Clinical Psychology*, **65**(5), 834-847.

Koss, Mary P. (1998). Hidden rape: sexual aggression and victimization in a national sample of students in higher education. In Burgess, A.W., (Ed). *Rape and Sexual Assault II.* New York: Garland, 3-25.

Koss, M.P., Hiese, L. & Russo, N.F. (1994). The global health burden of rape. Psychology of Women Quarterly, **18**, *509-537.*

Kozol, J. (1991). *Savage Inequalities.* New York: Crown Publishers.

Lisak, D. (1991). "Sexual aggression, masculinity, and fathers". *Signs: Journal of Women in Culture and Society.* **16**(2), 238-262.

Lisak, D., Hopper, J. & Song, P. (1996). Factors in the cycle of violence: Gender rigidity and emotional constriction. *Journal of Traumatic Stress*, **9**(4), 721-743.

Masters, J. J. (1997). *Finding Freedom: Writings from Death Row.* Junction City CA: Dharma Books, Padma Publishing.

Men Can Stop Rape (2007). Retrieved February 25, 2007 from web site: http://www.mencanstoprape.org/.

Miller, T. R., Cohen, M. A. & Wiersema, B. (1996). Victim Costs and Consequences: A New Look. Washington, D.C: U.S. Department of Justice, National Institute of Justice.

Nathanson, A. I. (1999). Identifying and explaining the relationship between parental mediation and children's aggression. *Communication Research*, **26** (2), 124-143.

O'Sullivan, C. (1991). Acquaintance gang rape on campus. In, Parrot, A and Bechhofe, L., (Eds.). *Acquaintance Rape: The Hidden Crime.* New York: John Wiley & Sons, 140-156.

Paynter, S. (2004, June 18). Refuse to look the other way. *Seattle Post Intelligencer,* F-6.

Resnick, H.S., Acierno, R., & Kilpatrick, D.G. (1997). Health impact of interpersonal violence: Medical and mental health outcomes. Behavioral Medicine, **23**, *65-78.*

Sanday, P. R. (1981). The socio-cultural context of rape: a cross-cultural study. *Journal of Social Issues.* **37**(4), 5-27.

Scott-Heron, G. (1975). "Winter in America" in, *The Best of Gil Scott-Heron.* New York: Arista Records.

Shé, E. (2002). It's about you, man. *Evergreen: The Evergreen State College Magazine,* **23**(1), 12-13.

Snyder, H. (2000). Sexual assault of young children as reported to law enforcement; Victim, incident, and offender characteristics. Washington D.C: National Center for Juvenile Justice. NCJJ182990, 17 pages.

Stoltenberg, J. (1990). *Refusing to Be a Man*. New York: Penguin-Mandarin.

Thompson, S. (2005). The 4 Cs of Sexual Aggression Avoidance Program. Mt. Pleasant, MI: Central Michigan University.

Thich Nhat Hanh (1991). *Peace Is Every Step*. New York: Bantam Books.

Tjaden, P. & Thoennes, N. (2000). The National Violence Against Women Survey (NVAWS), 2000. Washington D.C: National Institute of Justice and the Centers for Disease Control and Prevention, 68 pages.

Univ. of Texas-Austin (1992). Becoming Whole Again: Healing from Sexual Assault (1992). Mental Health Center, [Brochure].

Waldner-Haugrud, L. K. & Gratch, L. V. (1997). Sexual coercion in gay/lesbian relationships: descriptives and gender differences. *Violence and Victims*, **12**(1), 87-98.

Warshaw, R. (1994). *I Never Called It Rape*. New York: Harper and Row.

West, C. (2001). *Race Matters*. New York: Vintage Press.

MVP Music Lessons

The following classroom lessons are designed for educators who want to incorporate the music of popular culture into their violence prevention programs. A musical approach is both an enlightening and fun way to engage and involve students in prevention education. Our lesson plans accompany the MVP/Gear Up with Music curriculum described in Chapter 3.

MVP music can be used in a variety of ways to increase awareness of the issues that underpin sexual violence, abuse, racism, sexism and homophobia. Begin by either reviewing specific songs or the entire music CD before using it with students. Some teachers regard the CD/lessons as a "Songbook" from which to choose songs. Determine which songs are most appropriate for your students and your educational objectives. For optimal listening to the high quality sound of these songs use a stereo or CD boom box versus a computer, which may diminish sound quality due to small speaker size. The instrumental music CD is designed for students to craft their own MVP songs.

MVP music created by your students can be used in classroom discussions, as school PA announcements and for teacher and peer educator training. New ways to use this music continue to emerge. Be creative and experiment with its potential in your setting. Please let me know of your successes and the songs your students create!

To hear song samples or order the music CD's go to

www.todddennymvp.com

Activity #1

The Cards We Were Dealt

Purpose: To help students understand and appreciate individual differences in their ethnicity, race, gender and social class.

Materials: The CD song: "The Cards We Were Dealt"
A CD player
Large sheets of paper and markers

Lesson:

1. Discuss with students how we were all born with different "cards" based on our ethnicity, race, gender and social class.

2. Play the CD song "The Cards We Were Dealt."

3. Ask students to comment on some of the "cards" the musicians in the song were dealt. How did these "cards" impact the musicians' lives?

4. Ask students to comment on the "cards" they were dealt in their own lives.

5. Help students to understand how the "cards" they were dealt have either helped them or created challenges in their lives.

6. Lead students in a discussion of how the "cards" they were dealt might put them at risk for violence.

7. Discuss how these "cards" might be directly related to violence. For example girls are more likely to be victims of sexual harassment. Boys are more likely to be bullies. Young men are at highest risk for being a violent criminal offender.

Variation:

1. Put students in teams of four to five members. Have them brainstorm and write the "cards" they were dealt on large sheets of paper with markers. Ask them to look for similarities that group members share. What differences do the group members have?

2. Ask them to discuss and write down examples of famous people who have overcome difficult "cards" on the way to succeed in life.

3. Have each group share their large-sheet thoughts. Post the worksheets around the room or in the hallways.

4. Ask students to interview other students about the "cards" they were dealt. Encourage students to discuss how their "cards" have impacted their lives both positively and negatively.

5. Encourage students to think about how to overcome challenges based on ethnicity, race, gender and social class.

6. Have students watch the video "Tough Guise" to learn more about masculinity and violence.

   Contact: Media Education Foundation **info@mediaed.org**

   60 Masonic Street. Northampton, Massachusetts 01060

   Phone: (800) 897-0089 or (413) 584-8500

7. Have each team create a song based on their discussions and topic notes. Ask a team to volunteer to perform its song live to the class. Offer extra credit as an incentive.

Activity #2

Homophobia

Purpose: To help students understand how anti-gay beliefs and behaviors contribute to violence and also limit their own personal freedom.

Materials: The CD song, "Homophobia"
A CD player
Large sheets of paper and markers

Lesson:

1. Discuss how homophobia and anti-gay beliefs and behaviors contribute to violence in our schools and communities. Explain that homophobia limits the personal expression of all people.

2. Play the CD song "Homophobia".

3. Ask students to speculate on what reactions his friends might have if he chose to be a figure skater vs. being a hockey player. Is there a difference? If so, why?

4. Ask students to think about how homophobia effects both boys' and girls' choices of activities and actions in

our culture. What hobbies or professions have gay bias associated with them for men and women?

5. Ask students for examples that relate to the song "homophobia"; where their own freedom to choose a personal interest was limited by gay bias?

6. Ask students about the connection between homophobia and teen suicide. [Encourage them to recall key points raised in the song.]

7. What are the most common forms of homophobia students recognize in their own school and community? Are they the same or different? Why?

Variation

1. Group students in teams of four to five members. Have them write on large sheets of paper any ways they have become less homophobic and more accepting of differences in their own lives. Ask them to discuss and document ways they could increase their acceptance of differences in other people's lives and reduce homophobia.

2. Ask students to discuss what specific activities/actions would reduce homophobia and increase respect for gays in their school? In their community?

3. Have each group share their written, large-sheet thoughts. Post the worksheets around the room or in the hallways.

4. Ask each student to write a personal statement about how to reduce anti-gay bias.

5. Have students find examples of famous gay people in the library or on the Internet. What were they famous for? Explore why it is often more acceptable to admire these famous people than gay people in their own community.

6. Watch the video "It's Elementary."

    Women's Educational Media. 2180 Bryant Street, Suite 203 San Francisco, CA 94110. 415-641-4616 / 1-800-405-3322

7. For more information. Safe Schools Coalition, 1002 E. Seneca. Seattle, WA 98122-4203 / (206) 957-1621

8. Have each team create a song based their discussions and topic notes. Ask a team to volunteer to perform its song live to the class. Offer extra credit as an incentive.

Activity #3

Sticks and Stones

Purpose: To help students understand the impact of verbal abuse on school climate and the victim. To enhance school climate by creating alternatives to using harmful language and putdowns.

Materials: The CD song, "Sticks and Stones"
A CD player
Large sheets of paper and markers

Lesson:

1. Explain to your students that words can hurt as much as hands. Verbal abuse and putdowns often bring emotional pain and tears. Hurtful words can leave one feeling bruised inside.

2. Play the CD song "Sticks and Stones."

3. Discuss how sometimes the intent of the verbally abusive person is to make a joke or impress their friends.

4. Compare and contrast the intent of the verbally abusive person with the impact this has on the receiver of the

"Words." How does it feel to be in the 'shoes' of the recipient of the putdown?

5. Ask students to comment on how the abusive words in the song might impact students in their school.

6. Discuss how verbal abuse/putdowns can escalate into violence.

7. Explain that verbal abuse is the most common form of sexual harassment.

8. Share that, nationally, three of the top recipients of school sexual harassment are:

   * Girls who are physically well developed

   * Girls who are different, atypical or don't fit in with the crowd

   * Boys who are different or don't fit into the crowd

Variation:

1. Ask the students to discuss and write down examples of famous people who have overcome harassment to succeed in life.

2. Group students into teams of four to five members. Encourage the students to brainstorm and develop a "Words Are Not for

Hurting" ad campaign for their school. Write their ideas on the large sheets of paper with magic markers.

3. Have each group share its large-sheet thoughts. Post the worksheets around the room and in the hallways.

4. Ask students to interview another student about one thing they have already done to challenge or stop harassment. Was it a verbal or physical action?

5. Encourage students to explore non-violent interventions to stop verbal abuse.

6. Have each team create a song based on their discussions and topic notes. Ask if a group will perform its song live to the class. Offer extra credit as an incentive.

Activity #4

Jackie Robinson and Prejudice

Purpose: To inspire students to become more understanding and tolerant of racial differences.

Materials: The CD song "Courage II."
A CD player
Large sheets of paper and markers

Lesson:

1. Remind students of their different cultures, ethnic and racial backgrounds.

2. Play the CD song "Courage II."

3. Ask students to comment on the different backgrounds of Pee Wee Reese and Jackie Robinson. How did racial differences impact the baseball players' careers and lives?

4. Have students comment on major league baseball teams' racial makeup in the 1947 season. Was it different then compared with today? How?

5. Ask students to discuss the challenges Jackie faced as the first African American player in the major leagues. Did it take courage? Why?

6. What was the big turning point in Jackie's career? Did Pee Wee Reese take a risk? Would you define his action as courage?

Variation:

1. Have students get into groups of four to five members. Have each group document the race and ethnicity of its members. Look for similarities group members share.

2. Ask the students to discuss whether most of their friends are from their own racial background. If so, why? Is it difficult to accept others who are different from themselves? Why?

3. Discuss what it is like to be in a group that is in the racial majority. Next discuss what it feels like to be in a group that is the racial minority.

4. Encourage students to discuss if they have ever felt discriminated against -and why.

5. Have them brainstorm and write down examples of famous people who have overcome racial prejudice to succeed in life. What were they know for?

6. Watch the video "The Heart Knows Better."

   Imagery Film Ltd. NYC (212) 243-5579. E-mail address is IFL@mindspring.com 91 Bedford Street Suite 1R, New York, NY 10014

7. Have each team create a song based on their discussions and topic notes. Ask a group to volunteer to perform its song live to the class. Offer extra credit as an incentive.

Activity #5

Courage

Purpose: To challenge students to think about courage in positive and life affirming ways.

Materials: The CD song "Courage"
A CD player
Large sheets of paper and markers

Lesson:

1. Explain to students that courage is usually defined in terms of cultural socialization and stereotypes.

2. Play the CD song "Courage."

3. Ask students to comment on some of the positive expressions of courage in the song.

4. How are these expressions reflected in their own lives? (In their school and community.)

5. Can Mark McGuire's action be considered male courage? Why?

6. Ask the students to think of male traits that we consider to be courageous that might also be harmful and abusive? Can they think of female traits that we consider to be courageous? Are these similar or different from men's?

7. Ask students how some male expressions of courage might put them at risk for violence.

8. Explain that these sex role stereotypes are directly related to violence. Boys are more likely to be aggressive, dominant, in control and abusive. Boys are often the physical bully at school and are suspended and expelled more often then girls.

Variation:

1. Randomly assign students into groups of four to five. On the large sheets of paper and with markers have them brainstorm and develop a list of different socialized qualities of boys vs. girls. How are boys expected to act or behave in our culture? Contrast this with girls. Develop lists of actions and behaviors that are seen as inappropriate for boys and girls.

2. Ask students to discuss if these sex roles are acquired through culture and socialization – or do they think they are inborn?

3. Have them discuss the challenges to break out of these limiting sex roles. What makes it difficult?

4. Can students recall a time when they tried something others considered to be inappropriate for their gender role. Was this a challenge? Why?

5. Were there benefits of taking the risk? Were there repercussions?

6. Have each team create a song based on their discussions and topic notes. Ask a team to volunteer to perform its song live to the class. Offer extra credit as an incentive.

Activity #6

Choices

Purpose: To encourage students to examine life's challenges and personal choices in helping someone who is at risk of sexual harassment or aggression.

Materials: The CD song "Choices"
A CD player
Large sheets of paper and markers

Lesson:

1. Explain to students that when presented with difficult life choices we may feel unable take helpful action.

2. Play the CD song "Choices."

3. Ask students to comment on how they would feel if they observed the situation portrayed in the song. How would they feel if they were the women?

4. What are some of the challenges in this situation? What are you thinking and feeling? What might happen if you were to try to help the women?

5. Ask students to comment on the date rape drugs mentioned in the song. Ask what is the top date rape drug? Why?

6. Ask students how the situation would change if the woman in the song were their friend? Ask how they might feel if she were their sister?

7. What preventative actions can men take in this situation? What precautions do women need to take in this situation?

8. Ask students for a personal example of a sexual aggression situation in which they intervened. What actions did they take? Were they physical or cognitive? Was it helpful?

Variation:

1. Assign students to groups of four to five. Have them discuss and list the challenges in this situation on the large sheets of paper and with their markers. What makes it difficult to help the women in trouble?

2. Ask them to brainstorm and document non-violent interventions they could take to help the woman.

3. Have each group share their large sheet thoughts and actions. Post the worksheets around the room.

4. Have each student team review on the Internet a specific date rape drug (including, alcohol, Rohypnol, GHB and Ketamine) and report their finding to the class.

5. Have each team create a song based on their discussions and topic notes. Ask a team to volunteer to perform its song live to the class. Offer extra credit as an incentive.

Activity #7
Had a Drink

Purpose: To increase student's awareness of the potential consequences that one night of drinking can have.

Materials: The CD song "Had a Drink"
A CD player
Large sheets of paper and markers

Lesson:

1. Explain to students that alcohol is a huge contributing factor to many societal problems including sexually transmitted diseases and infections.

2. Play the CD song "Had a Drink."

3. Ask students to comment on why they think people like to drink alcohol.

4. Why do some people choose to not drink?

5. Ask students to comment on some of the sexually transmitted diseases and infections mentioned in the song.

6. Ask students how the situation might change if there were no alcohol involved?

7. What precautions do women need to take in this situation? What is the role of men in this situation? Do both genders share an equal responsibility in this scenario? Why or why not?

8. What are the safe sex techniques described in the song? What is the safest sex? (Discuss abstinence)

Variation:

1. Assign students into groups of four to five members each. Have them brainstorm and discuss what makes sex safe. What makes unsafe sex? Document their discussions on the large sheets of paper with markers

2. Have the student groups review the following topics on the Internet:

    * The different effects alcohol has on women vs. men.

    * Are men or women more vulnerable to alcohol's effects?

    * What is the difference between a sexually transmitted disease and infection?

    * What is the known relationship between alcohol and sexual assault?

- What are other health risks of alcohol?

3. Have each group share their large-sheet thoughts and their Internet findings.

4. Review the groups' findings and post the worksheets in the room.

5. Contact your area Planned Parenthood office to schedule a presentation by a community educator.

6. Have each team create a song based on their discussions and topic notes. Ask a team to volunteer to perform its song live to the class. Offer extra credit as an incentive.

Activity #8

Men Stopping Rape

Purpose: To encourage students to examine the attitudes and beliefs that support so-called "Deserving Rape Victim" characteristics; and to explore the role of sexual assault prevention for men and women.

Materials: The CD song "Men Stopping Rape"
A CD player
Large sheets of paper and markers

Lesson:

1. Discuss with the students how we all would say rape is wrong – but there are certain double standards that condone and perpetuate sexual violence.

2. Play the CD song.

3. Ask students to comment on the harmful attitudes and behaviors some men show towards women in our culture. What are some of their positive attributes?

4. What is the important distinction and difference between rape and romance?

5. Ask students to name the three so-called “Deserving Rape Victim” characteristics described in the song.

6. Discuss the concept of a double standard.

7. Ask students if there is a double standard relating to alcohol use by men vs. alcohol use by women? Are men at the same risk for being the victim of sexual violence if they use alcohol?

8. Discuss issues related to our choice of clothes. Why do some women dress in ways that guys would consider sexy or promiscuous? Are men at risk of sexual violence if they dress in similar ways?

9. What is the role for men in stopping rape? And the role for women? Is there an equal responsibility in rape prevention? Should men take a greater role in prevention? Why or why not?

10. Explain the legal definition of rape (see MSR chapter 6)

Variation:

1. Place girls in groups of four to five; repeat for boys. Have the boys discuss and document, using large sheets of paper and their markers, key words for what our culture reinforces for being a “Real Man.” Have the girls do the same for being a “Real Woman” in our culture.

2. Next post the two sheets on the wall side by side. Ask the class to brainstorm and discuss how these different sex-role stereotypes might contribute to sexual violence. Examine and contrast key words for both genders.

3. Have them examine how alcohol and dress relate to their gender roles.
   What are the differences? Are their similarities?

4. Have each group share its written, large-sheet thoughts. Post the worksheets around the room.

5. Contact your area Community Sexual Assault/Domestic Violence agency to schedule a presentation.

6. Have each team create a song based on their discussions and topic notes. Ask a team to volunteer to perform its song live to the class. Offer extra credit as an incentive.

Activity # 9

"Hands Are Not for Hurting"

Purpose: To help students understand the warning signs in an abusive relationship; and to distinguish between a healthy and abusive relationship.

Materials: The CD song "Hands Are Not for Hurting"
A CD player
Large sheets of paper and markers

Lesson:

1. Explain to students that a healthy relationship does not involve jealousy, control or mental/physical abuse. Relationship violence commonly begins with controlling actions, verbal/emotional abuse and escalates into physical abuse.

2. Listen to the CD song "Hands Are Not for Hurting" or watch the video go to www.olywa.net/tdenny

3. Ask if Jimmy had a right to be jealous in this situation? Why or why not?

4. Does he have a right to be violent to Susan?

5. What other options did Jimmy have besides being violent to handle the situation? Do you think Jimmy's anger is a problem or a normal reaction to the situation?

6. Was it OK for Susan to talk with her old boyfriend? Why or why not?

7. As a friend what could you do to help in this situation? Is it your business? Do your actions change if you don't know Jimmy or Susan?

8. Who else might be able to help Jimmy with this situation? Who might be able to help Susan with this situation?

Variation:

1. Group students by gender into teams of four to five members.

2. Have the class watch the video.

3. Ask the students to discuss the film. What were they thinking while they watched? How would they feel in the role of Susan or Jimmy? What makes it challenging in these respective roles?

4. Ask the groups to describe actions they could take to safely intervene if they witnessed this situation? How could they use their brains vs. physical violence to help? Would it be safer to tell an adult? Who could they approach for help?

5. Have the girls discuss the situation from Susan's perspective. What could they do if they were her in that situation? How could they get help?

6. Have the boys put themselves in the role of being a friend of Jimmy. What could they do to help him?

7. Have each team create a song based on their discussions and topic notes. Ask a team to volunteer to perform its song live to the class. Offer extra credit as an incentive.

Activity #10

Choices II

Purpose: To encourage students to examine life's challenges and personal choices in helping someone who is at risk of school harassment.

Materials: The CD song "Choices II"
A CD player
Large sheets of paper and markers

Lesson:

1. Discuss with the students how we can develop skills to help others who are being bullied or harassed.

2. Listed to the song, "Choices II."

3. Ask students to comment on the situation portrayed in the song. Is it common in their school? If so why? How would they feel if they were the victim?

4. What are some of the challenges as a bystander in this scenario? What are you thinking? What might happen if you were to try to help the student?

5. Ask students how the situation would change for them if the victim were their friend?

6. What prevention roles can students take in this situation? Would it be safer to tell an adult? Who could they tell?

7. Ask students to think of a personal example of a harassment situation they intervened in. What action did they take? Were they able to verbally diffuse the situation? How?

Variation:

1. After placing the students in groups of four to five, have them discuss and write with markers the challenges in this situation on the large sheets of paper. What makes it difficult to help the student in trouble?

2. Ask them to brainstorm and document non-violent interventions they could take to help.

3. Have each group share their large-sheet thoughts. Post the worksheets around the room after the discussion.

4. Have each student team search the library or Internet for information on school harassment/bullying and report it's finding to the entire class.

5. Have each team create a song based on their discussions and topic notes. Ask a team to volunteer to perform its song live to the class. Offer extra credit as an incentive.

A Call for Research on Male Violence Prevention Education

ALTHOUGH I AM FAMILIAR WITH the modest amount of research relating to sexual assault and male violence prevention, I am not terribly impressed with it. The sad truth is we have little evidence from research and evaluation that supports using one type of intervention over another. We do not know if we should focus our research on male groups such as athletes or fraternity members because they over-represent perpetrators of sexual assault and because of their stature and influence with other men. We do not know the length of time required for our programs to positively change men's values about sexual violence or which approaches will keep men involved in sustained programs. Nor do we know the proportion of men who are or have been abusive. Who among our young men stand the greater chance of being involved in and benefiting the most from our programs?

It is apparent and disturbing to me that we don't know which of our interventions are successful or unsuccessful. Our field has practitioners who work hard, think they make a difference, and are in need of evaluative information. We have crucial questions that must be answered if we are to be more successful in addressing the continuing challenge of male violence.

I am not calling for research or evaluation that will identify "the way" to teach violence prevention to males. The reasons underlying success in one program cannot necessarily be generalized to programs elsewhere. Education is more complex than raising corn or building Toyotas. Replication and generalization are possible in agriculture and the automobile industry; but in the field of education, we are unable to generalize about program effectiveness within the same town, much less across the nation. Every campus and community has distinct nuances and characteristics. Nevertheless we at least should know about and examine the parameters of successful programs wherever they exist.

Our work addresses young men's concepts of masculinity as shaped by family and our culture. I suspect that our interventions change men's beliefs and behaviors toward violence against women to the extent that we help them address that key concept. If I am correct, which factors in our workshops, in our training, and in our follow-up account for the changes we produce? To put it plainly: we do not know as much as we should. What we do know is that we have a large problem and an inadequate response on the part of educational institutions in particular and society in general.

I created a program of intervention that makes use of popular culture (Gear Up with Music). The program uses music to carry the message of nonviolence to K-12 students. Does it work? It seems to me that it does; the students truly immerse themselves into the week-long residency and praise it. But neither I nor my colleagues have conducted studies to establish the validity of our impressions for any of our programs; nor do we have longitudinal studies or external evaluations that have established the effects of our programs.

How many Columbine High School tragedies, Virginia Tech mass murders, churchman abusing children travesties, and male professional sports scandals will it take to raise our national awareness to the level where we take seriously the widespread practice of male violence against women? We need well-funded, well-designed studies of these matters and of our interventions as well. I am less concerned with high-profile scandals reported by our media and more concerned with the millions of unreported cases of sexual assault and domestic violence that occur across our nation. My work has taken me throughout the United States to scores of colleges, schools, and prisons, where I have seen first-hand how widespread male violence continues to be in our nation. We need to create effective interventions and we need to find them soon.

I am a practitioner—not a researcher. I have a master's degree in social work with concentrations in mental health and school curricula. Although research is the appropriate role for those in the academy, I think it is incumbent on practitioners to evaluate the results of their work. We need a normative database that considers the respondents' backgrounds, gender, ethnicity, sexual orientation and life experiences to examine the results of our programs.

I rarely present a program without evaluating it. Over the past two decades I have gathered thousands of evaluative responses of my work. All workshop participants have the potential to profit from my program and to contribute to improving it through their evaluative responses. I continue to perfect a series of interventions that an independent audit of my evaluations indicates are effective. I take seriously the criticisms and evaluations that I receive from students, faculty, and colleagues. Although I appreciate kudos and high praise, I am especially interested in participants who do not respond enthusiastically to my efforts. They often give me new insights for revising and improving the programs. (This book, for example, will produce critical appraisals from which I will learn as well.) All this is good, but practice should be informed by solid, educational research.

An illustrative research proposal to study the effectiveness of male intervention programs at a public institution of higher education follows.

A Research Proposal to Survey College Males' Attitudes about Violence toward Women:

Sexual violence on campus is an issue of increasing concern. Despite the incidence and profound social importance of the problem, little is known about the beliefs that young men of college age hold toward acts of violence committed toward women. What is known is largely anecdotal in nature. Campus programs that intervene in the socialization of men, such as a Men's Violence Prevention program, if they are to be successful, should begin earlier than the college years. The U.S. Department of education should create grants for K-12 campus violence prevention against girls. In the absence of earlier interventions, however, higher education would appear to be an appropriate arena for such programs. To base a new intervention on something other than conventional wisdom and to augment our meager empirical data, we propose a research program to examine extant male attitudes toward sexual violence. The study would be restricted to a sample of male student social groups attending the college during their academic careers.

Sexual assault occurs widely on our college campuses, is rarely prosecuted, is described as being something other than rape, and continues to be a part of institutional attitudes that both privileges men and victimizes women. It is vital to any college or university to make discernible progress in reducing campus rape. As a public institution, our college has the responsibility to assure parents of the safety of their daughters who attend this campus. At the most cursory, political level, it is clearly in the enlightened self-interest of the college to put forth the image of being a caring institution.

To address the issue of rape on this campus it is crucial that we have better insight into male attitudes and beliefs regarding violence toward women. The strength of this proposed research lies, at a minimum, in its development of an assessment strategy to gather data and to act as a catalyst for increasing effectiveness of preventive programs directed at issues related to male sexual violence. The data are intended to reveal factors that contribute to gender violence on our campus. Maximally the study could contribute to the development and validation of a program for reducing campus sexual assault.

Specifically, this study intends to examine the effectiveness of an intervention aimed at changing male beliefs regarding violent sexual acts on women. If it proves to be an effective means of reducing campus rape, the implications for continuing and expanding the program further would be clear. A lesser but nonetheless worthy goal would be to determine the utility of the proposed survey instrument to identify groups of men who appear to need the most help with their sexual attitudes toward women. If the survey instrument can be demonstrated to reliably discriminate high (i.e., most likely to hold violent attitudes) from low groups, other interventions beyond our program could be tried and subsequently measured by such an instrument.

Such a proposal would also describe the study's research design, the nature of the sample, the instrumentation to be used and the statistics appropriate for the data. I feel certain that sophisticated researchers could readily improve the design of this study. For example, the unique, longitudinal study conducted by John Foubert (2000) is meritorious in spite of its limitations. The research community should be doing much more of this kind of work.

What will be the results of your using material that you might adapt from this book? Will your findings corroborate or challenge mine? I'd like to know. We need carefully designed studies that exclude the errors that may have crept into our efforts. We need to learn what works and what does not in the field of male violence prevention education. For now, let's exchange information with each another about what seems to be successful.

The stakes are too high to avoid addressing the need for research and evaluation on what makes a difference in preventing gender violence. Similarly, we cannot delay our practice while waiting for the research community to join us. There should be no excuse that money is unavailable for such studies. I would guess that each year, less money is spent nationally on research and evaluation of programs designed to reduce male violence than is spent to incarcerate rapists in the state of Washington alone (in 2001, that included $19 million for a sex-offender commitment center and $103 million dollars for incarcerating sexual predators).

What are the underlying variables that contribute to successful men's violence prevention programs? In the absence of research findings doesn't it make sense to share success stories?

DURING THE PAST TWO DECADES, Todd Denny has conducted over a thousand workshops and training programs for colleges, universities, public schools, professional conferences and community organizations across the nation.

He was featured in the award-winning PBS documentary "*Date Rape: a Different Set of Rules.*"

Todd also designed and implemented a ground-breaking MVP music program that attracts students to the work of violence prevention.

Todd pioneered Men's Violence Prevention (MVP) programs at:

* The Evergreen State College
* The University of Illinois

His programs have been funded by the U.S. Department of Education's Gear-Up Program, Upward Bound, The National Science Foundation and the National Geographic Society.

He lives in Olympia, WA

For more information see www.todddennymvp.com

Or call Todd at (360) 866-7140

www.ingramcontent.com/pod-product-compliance
Ingram Content Group UK Ltd.
Pitfield, Milton Keynes, MK11 3LW, UK
UKHW040602210726
13854UKWH00008B/1831